DACHSHUND

FROM THE EDITORS OF DOGFANCY MAGAZINE

Dachshund, a Smart Owner's Guide™
part of the Kennel Club Books® Interactive Series™
ISBN: 978-1-593787-66-0 ©2009
Kennel Club Books Inc., 40 Broad St., Freehold, NJ 07728. Printed in South Korea. All rights reserved. No part of this book may be reproduced in any form, by Photostat, scanner, microfilm, xerography, or any other means, or incorporated into any information retrieval system, electronic or mechanical, without the written permission of the copyright owner.

photographers include Tara Darling, Isabelle Français, Carol Ann Johnson, Alice van Kempen, John Merriman, and Bill Tacke; contributing writer: Charlotte Schwartz

W elcome to the wonderful world of Dachsies. Whether you're just learning about this versatile breed or already have one in your life, you're in for a good time.

A Dachshund will enjoy outings with you, challenge you a bit, and snuggle up to you at night. This breed is a perfect take-along dog. Not as small as many companion breeds, your low-to-the-ground dog is a sturdy fellow who may have a smooth, wirehaired, or long coat. You also have the choice of a miniature or standard size, as well as a variety of colors. That's a lot of options for a single breed.

While some small dogs are quite submissive to their owners, you'll find your Dachsie to be a bit independent. Balancing this is his absolute, unquestionable love for treats. Your smart dog will quickly learn that when he can figure out what you want him to do, he gets a yummy goody.

As you train your new dog, you'll see that he's a sensitive fellow as well. He can't understand why you would ever raise your voice to him. And he insists that you greet him when you come home—whether you've been away all day or just for an hour. In turn, he will welcome you with his energetic, wildly wagging tail, and a look in his eyes that can only be interpreted as true love.

Do nothing to disappoint him, and he will try his very best to do the same. When he makes mistakes, ignore them, move on, and work on your training techniques. When your Dachsie fails, it's because you haven't quite gotten him to understand yet. But he will.

Using treats to train your pal is great. But buy healthy ones that you can break into tiny bits, or use pieces of vegetables or fruit. One of the Dachsie's downfalls is his tendency to gain weight. If you feed him healthy meals, watch the treats, and don't give in when his eyes plead for fatty people food, you'll be fulfilling one of your most important responsibilities.

Diet alone won't keep this wonderful breed in good health. He also needs exercise. Not as much as other breeds, but enough to get his heart racing and his little legs pumping, and to spread that crazy grin that Dachsies get when they run full out. Two 15-minute walks a day, plus a run at the dog park, a game of fetch, or a few dashes up and down the hall chasing a ball a few times a week will keep him lean and muscular.

Dachshunds were designed to go after small animals, and they still have that urge to chase. If your cat doesn't like a good run, you will need to teach your new pup that's not OK. Keep him on a leash whenever you go outside. Otherwise, he'll take off after the first squirrel, cat, or bird he sees. The upside of this trait is that he'll love playing with a small stuffed animal that he thinks of as prey. Chasing this critter and tearing into it will use up some of his energy before bedtime.

There's one other thing you must do for your Dachsie. Give him a step to get up onto your couch and bed—if he's allowed. Lift him in and out of your car. His long back makes him susceptible to back injuries. But with these simple preventive steps and regular exercise, you can help keep his back healthy.

This sounds like a lot of work, but once you get your Dachshund home, he'll quickly

JOIN OUR ONLINE **Dachsie Club**

With this Smart Owner's Guide™, you are well on your way to getting your Dachsie diploma. But your Dachshund education doesn't end here. You're invited to join Club Dachsie™ (**DogChannel.com/Club-Dachsie**), a FREE online site with lots of fun and instructive online features like:

◆ **forums, blogs,** and **profiles** where you can connect with other Dachsie owners
◆ **downloadable charts** and **checklists** to help you be a smart and loving Dachsie owner
◆ access to **e-cards, wallpapers,** and **screensavers**
◆ interactive **games**
◆ Dachsie-specific **quizzes**

The **Smart Owner's Guide™** series and Club Dachsie™ are backed by the experts at DOG FANCY magazine and DogChannel.com—who have been providing trusted and up-to-date information about dogs and dog people for forty years. Log on and join the club today!

worm his way into your heart. Everything you do with him will be fun: training, walks, trips to the pet-supply store, baths, car rides, and just relaxing together on the couch.

He's already devoted to you. All you have to do is lap it up, and enjoy every minute!

Susan Chaney
Editor, DOG FANCY

THE DACHSIE

Saying you want a Dachshund is similar to going into a candy store and saying you want some chocolate. There are many kinds of chocolates, and many kinds of Dachshunds. They come in two different sizes and three coat types, each with its own characteristics and group of devoted owners and admirers.

Standard Dachshunds tip the scales at 16 to 32 pounds, while miniature Dachshunds weigh in at just 11 pounds or less. The three coat types are smooth (the coat is smooth and shining), wirehaired (body is covered with a short, thick, uniform outer coat with a finer, softer undercoat), and longhaired (long, wavy hair).

Dachshunds come in a variety of colors, too. Common colors are red, black and tan, gray and fawn. They also come in some coat patterns like dappled and brindle.

This versatile breed is often described as being extroverted with the ability to act the fool on occasion. He is clever, lively, and courageous. Because he is small in size, he is easy to maintain in good physical condition and doesn't require long runs. Possessing a friendly, companion-

it's a
Fact

There are six varieties of Dachshunds:
- standard smooth
- standard longhaired
- standard wirehaired
- miniature smooth
- miniature longhaired
- miniature wirehaired

This breed comes in three coat types: smooth, longhaired and wirehaired (right).

able personality, the Dachshund charms his way into the hearts of all who get to know him.

However, the Dachshund is a hound and hunter at heart and is naturally curious. He will investigate everything he finds, which means he likes to chew on things—a lot.

Make sure to keep your dog occupied with a variety of interesting and interactive chew toys. He has badger hunting instincts, so don't be surprised by his proclivity for digging—in the yard and in your home. Make sure your Dachshund cannot escape your yard by digging under fences; he's small and low and can get under almost anything!

Dachshunds are incredibly loyal. They love people, especially children and the elderly, and should be included in everyday activities. When left alone or ignored, Dachshunds are likely to suffer from separation anxiety.

It's not surprising that Dachshunds are among the most popular dog breeds in the United States, Germany, and Britain. Although the original purpose of hunting is no longer the main reason to own Dachshunds, they possess so many other desirable qualities that they undoubtedly will retain their popular status for many years to come.

The miniature is mature by twelve months of age, while the standard may not be fully mature until he is eighteen months old. Dachshunds are exceptionally long-lived dogs, with many living to be twelve to fourteen years old. Regardless of size or variety, the Dachsie is easily maintained and managed.

THE HEALTH OF THIS HOUND

The peculiar and unique body structure of your Dachshund makes him prone to back problems. Do not let him jump on or leap off high places like couches and beds, which is easier said than done because Dachshunds can be rather stubborn at times. Behavior easily can be modified by a smart owner who quickly gets his dog to focus on some new activity. In other words, you must refuse to recognize the Dachshund's obstinacy and thereby prevent a repetition of the undesirable behavior. Physical rough handling only makes an even-tempered Dachshund become aggressive.

Generally speaking, most dogs are square creatures, about as high from the ground to the top of their shoulders as

Did You Know?

There is some variation in the personality among Dachshund coat types. Generally speaking:
- Longhaireds are more laidback.
- Wirehaireds are social clowns.
- Smooths are more intense and stubborn.

SMART TIP!

Don't forget that Dachshunds are scenthounds. That means they will go where their noses tell them to go! When on walks, keep them on leash, and if you have a backyard, build a good fence.

they are from the front of their chests to their rumps. Each of their four legs is placed directly under the trunk of the body at the four corners. Their necks are gently arched and their heads balance out their body size: little heads for little dogs,

big heads for big dogs. Dachshunds, however, are different. Their long, low-to-the-ground body type resembles a train with an engine in the front, a caboose at the end and the cars in the middle. Their long, swaying tails even add to their length, to accentuate how very different they are!

Because of their unique skeletal structure, Dachshunds have the potential to experience environmental and genetic problems common to long-bodied dogs. Living in an environment that is oblivious to their special conformation, Dachshunds

Just like not all days are rainy days, not all Dachsies are alike.

often are subjected to many hazards. Jumping, excessive stair-climbing and other high-impact activities usually result in serious diseases and conditions of the vertebrae. When genetically inferior dogs are bred, they often produce genetically inferior puppies. These puppies, in turn, grow up to develop serious skeletal conditions that are difficult or impossible to correct. In addition, overweight dogs are always at risk.

It's important to note that not all Dachshunds will suffer serious physical diseases or problems. However, it is important for a smart buyer to be aware of the health conditions that can affect the dog he is about to purchase. Healthy parents and a well-informed, caring breeder are the best factors in producing healthy puppies.

Many health problems in dogs today can be tested for in very young puppies. Reputable breeders usually have these tests performed so that they can send their Dachshund puppies off to new homes with certificates of good health. Then, new owners can begin raising their puppy in the knowledge that they have chosen a healthy puppy from a quality source. In short, it all boils down to the old saying that knowledge is power—with humans, and with Dachshunds.

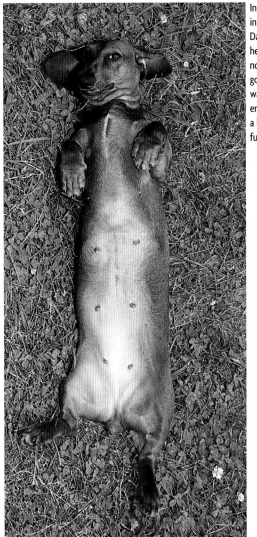

Investing in your Dachsie's health now will go a long way to ensure a brighter future.

WIENER PERSONALITY

If you have a friendly personality, you and your Dachshund will immediately have something in common. Dachshunds are social dogs who are always interested in doing fun things with *their* person. Indoor and outdoor games of fetch are of particular interest to them. Visits to the park and daily walks are much enjoyed by your little companion. Organized activities like obedience, agility and field trials also can be rewarding for both you and your Dachshund.

Your Dachsie is an intelligent companion with a strong character. You must make it clear to him that you are the boss. You must never be unkind or harsh, but a commanding tone of voice will be an asset. You will need to train your dog to be obedient, and

In a Dachshund, I look for self-confidence and a distinct personality. I want them to be outgoing and playful. I look for them to be proud and loyal. With positive reinforcement, Dachshunds can do no wrong. They are intelligent dogs and love to please their masters. They have a large-dog personality in a small-dog body.

—*Debra Coverdell, Dachshund breeder in Fairfield, Mont.*

his training should start while he is still young. Additionally, hours of enjoyment will be spent watching your Dachshund clown around and, if you are willing to join in with his games, he will be that much happier.

The Dachshund is a small breed, and you will find yourself fiercely devoted to the breed—just as the Dachshund is dedicated to you. It will be an advantage if you are fairly active, because as an adult, your Dachshund will enjoy a good walk each day. Although small, he is energetic! Of course, snuggling beneath the covers on a cold, rainy day is another favorite activity for your Dachshund.

Dachshunds do not like being left alone for long periods of time. They do best when they're mentally stimulated and made to

feel appreciated and treated like members of the family.

How do you know if a Dachshund is the right breed for you? It's the law of averages. A Dachshund is not one dog, but many: longhaired, wirehaired, and smooth; standard, miniature, and the "tweenies" that fall between standard and miniature. As for the color: It's been estimated that Dachshunds

True to their nature, Dachsies love to dig! If you like a nice, neat garden, then this breed may not be for you.

come in 176 colors, shades and tints. What's not to like?

If you want to get technical: Dachshunds are diggers. They made their living (historically, at least) by digging, and dig they will. If you prefer a boring, smooth, solid green lawn, perhaps the Dachshund is not for you. Even when the lawn is not in danger, your furniture might be.

If you like the strong, silent type, it won't be a Dachshund. Dachshunds are barkers. They alert quickly and are interested in sav-

Show your artistic side. Share photos, videos, and artwork of your favorite breed on Club Dachsie. You can also submit jokes, riddles, and even poetry about Dachshunds. Browse through our various galleries and see the talent of fellow Dachsie owners. Go to **DogChannel.com/Club-Dachsie** and click on "galleries" to get started.

JOIN OUR ONLINE
Dachsie Club

Dachshunds come in all sorts of colors, from solids with or without markings to dappled patterns.

SINGLE COLOR: Smooth and longhaired Dachsies may be any color: red, with or without dark or sable (black-tipped) hairs, and cream are just two examples of single-colored Dachshunds. Wirehaireds also may be any color. However, the predominant colors are wild boar (dull gray hairs intermingled with black hairs), black and tan, and shades of red.

TAN MARKINGS: Tan markings are acceptable on all coat types and may be found on black, chocolate, wild boar, gray (silver blue), and fawn Dachshunds, but they must not be too pale or too prominent. These markings are allowed over the eyes, on the sides of the jaw and underlip, on the inner edge of the ear, on the front and breast, inside and beside the front legs, and on the paws. The tan markings are also found around the anus, and from there, running up the underside of the tail to one-third to one-half the length of the tail.

DAPPLED PATTERNS: A single-dapple pattern consists of lighter-colored areas contrasting with a darker base color, which may be any acceptable color. In this pattern, neither the light nor the dark colors should be predominant. Partially or entirely blue eyes, which are called walleyes, are acceptable in this pattern. A large area of white on the chest is permissible.

A double-dapple pattern consists of varying amounts of white in addition to the dapple pattern. Partially or entirely self-colored nose (same color as the coat) and nails are acceptable. These dapple patterns are acceptable in smooth or longhaired varieties.

BRINDLE: The brindle pattern consists of black or dark stripes that are laid over a lighter color. This pattern is acceptable for smooth and longhaired Dachshunds. A small amount of white on the chest is acceptable, but not desirable.

The Dachshund comes in more than 170 different colors.

ing your neck from every passerby. But these are minor problems, surely.

Who wouldn't put up with a minefield in the lawn and a bit of barking for the pleasure of owing a Dachsie? Don't think of digging and barking as faults; the Dachshund is busy protecting you from badgers and burglars! Besides, these are minor idiosyncrasies that give further depth and quality to the breed.

THREE COATS, THREE PERSONALITIES

More than any other dog, it's difficult to generalize about the Dachshund personality. Dachshunds are so special that every coat type has a slightly different character. This was an accident of creation because breeders were looking for different kinds of coats and not different kinds of personali-

ties, but apparently certain temperament genes are connected to different coats, at least in this breed.

If you want the classic, regal, one-person type of dog, the smooth is for you. Somewhat aloof and less tolerant than his wiry and longhaired cousins, the smooth Dachshund is a classic example of what people mean when they say "Dachshund." Be aware, however, that of the three types, the smooth Dachshund is the most stubborn, even willful.

If your taste runs to laidback elegance, you can't do better than the handsome longhaired. Some Dachshund *aficionados* maintain that the long-haired variety actually makes the best hunter of the three types. But long coats mean lots of grooming to keep them looking their glorious best.

Like a clownish, friendly fella? That's the wirehaired—a marshmallow in armor. The wiry coat is almost shed free and makes the wirehaired the ideal choice for people who tend to have dog allergies. But you'd better have the energy to keep up with his relentless activity. And if you want your Dachsie to have the correct wire coat, it requires handstripping and a lot of patience.

A dappled Dachsie is a delight!

Longhaired Dachsies are known for being laidback and friendly.

Astrid loved her little, red rubber ball. When my partner, Bill, and I brought her home at twelve weeks of age, we gave her this ball to make her feel more confident in her surroundings, to know that she was loved. Being a very athletic, chocolate-smooth Dachshund, she took to it right away.

She became obsessed with it. She pounced on every opportunity to play "fetch" with anyone she deemed worthy—sometimes, for hours on end, if we let her. She would never let the ball out of her sight. In fact, she even tried to eat and drink with the ball still in her mouth! And, of course, the red ball was her pillow at night.

The little red ball became the center of her world, and she guarded it fiercely from our black-and-tan smooth Dachsie, a ten-year-old named Elsa. Every once in a while, Elsa tried to snatch the ball away, but Astrid never let her have it. Elsa could have any other toy, but never the little red ball.

Six years passed and Elsa neared her sixteenth birthday and became much weaker,

Bill and I discussed putting Elsa down. Then one morning, when Elsa woke up so sick and helpless, we knew it was time.

While we prepared ourselves to take her to the vet for the last time, Astrid did something she had never done before. With the little red ball in her mouth, she trotted from the other end of the house to where Elsa lie, and carefully placed the ball in front of Elsa, as if to say, "This ball makes me feel better; I hope it makes you feel better, too."

Elsa looked at Astrid with that recognition that only dogs know. She rested her head on the ball, and glanced at Astrid with a sort of quiet comfort.

We took the ball with us to the vet and it stayed with Elsa to the end.

A few months passed, and we were still getting over Elsa's loss when Bill was diagnosed with a malignant brain tumor. Now, more than ever, after the surgery and the radiation, Bill and Astrid wanted to play "fetch" with that little red ball. It became the focal point of their relationship.

When it was time for Bill to go into hospice, Astrid had to be left at home where she became terribly sad and anxious. Pacing and drooling, she looked for Bill with her ball in her mouth. I tried to engage her with a game of "fetch," but it wasn't the same. She longed for Bill.

Finally, I was given clearance to bring Astrid to the hospice, and, of course, she had her ball. She was much calmer now as we walked down the hall and approached Bill's room. Astrid was in my arms as we entered, and I set her down on his bed. They both melted when they saw each other. Astrid could sense how much weaker Bill was. He could no longer talk. Astrid quietly picked up the ball in her mouth and gently placed it on Bill's chest. She looked at him for a few seconds, and then proceeded to curl up at his side, nudging his arm around herself to fall asleep.

Astrid only got to see Bill once in the hospice, because he died the next day. But when I took her home, she was at peace. She didn't worry about Bill anymore. She knew where he was, and she knew he was safe. But most of all, Astrid knew that she had done her part by giving Bill her heart—the little red ball.

—John Merriman,
proud Dachshund owner

DACHSIE DOSSIER

This sweet, intelligent hound is short in stature but long on love.

COUNTRY OF ORIGIN: Germany

ALIASES: Dachsie, Teckel, Doxie, wiener dog, badger dog

SIZE: miniature—11 pounds or less; standard—16 pounds or more

COAT & COLOR: three coat types—smooth, wirehaired, longhaired. The most popular colors are solid red or black and tan, but the coat may be chocolate, gray or white with rust markings; dappled or brindle.

PERSONALITY TRAITS: spunky, brave, and hard working. Dachshunds were bred to dig badgers, foxes, and rodents from their underground dens, so that digging spirit still lives on, though most are content to be companion dogs.

WITH KIDS: gets along best with adults and older, responsible children

WITH OTHER PETS: good with other dogs if properly introduced. Dachsies may see smaller pets (such as rats and hamsters) as prey, so all interactions should be well supervised.

ENERGY LEVEL: high

EXERCISE NEEDS: Daily walks are a must for this breed, as well as regular play sessions.

GROOMING NEEDS: longhaired—daily combing and brushing; wirehaired—daily combing and brushing, as well as professional trimmings twice a year; smooth—weekly rubdown with a grooming mitt or damp cloth to remove dirt and keep the coat shiny.

TRAINING NEEDS: Dachsies are intelligent and quickly grasp training cues, but are stubborn and may not follow directions if they aren't given the proper incentive. Dachsies respond best to patient, persistent training. All Dachshunds should be taught the five basics cues: sit, lie down, stay, come, and heel.

LIVING ENVIRONMENT: These small, adaptable dogs can live equally well in an apartment or house, in the city, or in the country.

LIFESPAN: 12 to 15 years

Dachshunds are long-bodied, short-legged dogs—small in stature, but very large in personality—whose noses are so close to the ground that not much escapes their notice! In fact, their physical structure is the primary reason for their hunting expertise. The Dachsie's scenting ability was recognized by German hunters as early as the 15th century.

Derived from early German hounds known as Deutsche Bracken, these little dogs were called "badger dogs" or "diggers." Eventually they were crossed with small, terrier-type dogs to produce the Dachshunds we know today. With the nose of the hound, the long, low body that burrows into holes and the fearless terrier-like enthusiasm for the chase, the Dachshund is difficult to beat.

Early artistic illustrations and sculptures from the 15th, 16th and 17th centuries show Dachshund-type dogs hunting badgers. A statue of an early Egyptian pharaoh also has a Dachshund-type dog named "Teckel" on it. In each depiction, the characteristics of strength, stamina, courage, and keenness were clearly conveyed.

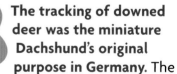

Did You Know?

The tracking of downed deer was the miniature Dachshund's original purpose in Germany. The miniature Dachshund used his fine nose and low-to-the-ground stature, making him an exceptional tracking dog.

Dachshunds come in two sizes: standard and miniature.

Originally, standard Dachshunds weighed between 30 and 35 pounds and were used in packs to catch wild boar. The modern-day Dachshund, however, weighs in at considerably less: 16 to 32 pounds.

Miniatures originally weighed 16 to 25 pounds and hunted fox or tracked wounded deer. Today, the average miniature weighs 8 to 12 pounds and hunts rabbit or hare. Occasionally, a miniature of only 5 to 6 pounds will be used in hunting, providing that the dog possesses plenty of hunting spirit that serves to offset his diminutive size.

There are three coat varieties in Dachshunds: smooth, longhaired and wirehaired. The smooth and longhaired varieties were developed first. The wirehaired variety was developed later for hunting in briars and thorn bushes.

Coat colors offer something for every Dachshund lover. Red, cream, bicolor, black, chocolate, wild boar, gray-blue, fawn, dappled, and brindle are colors and color combinations that can be found wherever Dachshunds are bred.

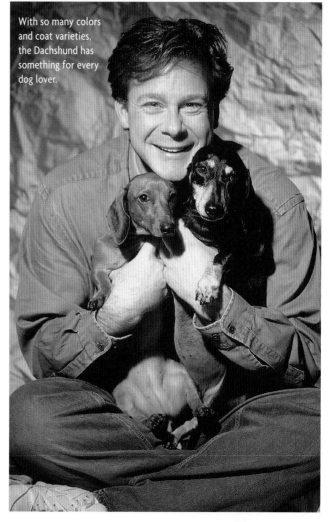

With so many colors and coat varieties, the Dachshund has something for every dog lover.

Regardless of size, coat, or color, all Dachsies possess exceptional scenting and digging abilities, which make them ideal hunters.

Did You Know?

A **breed standard** (also called bench standard) is a set of guidelines which a breeder uses to produce a single looking dog and which a conformation judge uses during a dog show. The standard typically lists the ideal size of a dog (height, weight), the colors his coat can be, temperament qualities, and more. To read the Dachshund standard, visit the **American Kennel Club** website, **www.akc.org**, and go to the Dachsie page.

Dachsies make good hunters because of their excellent sense of smell.

GERMAN INGENUITY

As with most breeds, it wasn't until the 19th century that breed and kennel clubs were formed and breeders began keeping organized records. The first German all-breed stud book, the *Deutscher Hunde-*

> ### it's a Fact
> **Newspaper magnate William Randolph Hearst owned Dachshunds.** At his home in San Simeon, overlooking the central California coast, a tiny ladder emerges from the swimming pool, placed there in case Hearst's Dachsie, Helen, fell in and couldn't get out.

Stammbuch, produced in 1840, recorded fifty-four Dachshunds. Dachshund hunting clubs also kept stud books that listed dogs with demonstrated hunting ability.

The Dachsie's development in Germany was guided in large part by Major Emil Ilgner, who founded many Dachshund clubs, and by Fritz Engelmann, who wrote a book called *Der Dachshund* (now out of print). The two men prized the breed for its working abilities, and bred for dogs who were low to the ground, with long, supple bodies and front legs and feet designed for digging.

German breeders wrote a standard for the Dachshund in 1879, and in 1888 they formed the German Dachshund Club (Deutscher Teckelklub). In 1915, German breeders began using initials with registration numbers to denote the dog's coat type. Smooths were

In Germany, the breed's name means "badger dog."

Just how quickly will your Dachshund puppy grow?
Go to Club Dachsie and download a growth chart. You also can see your pup's age in human years; the old standard of multiplying your dog's age by seven isn't quite accurate. Log onto **DogChannel.com/Club-Dachsie** and click on "downloads."

identified by a K (*kurzhaar*), wirehairs by an R (*rauhhaar*) and longhairs by an L (*langhaar*). The types were further delineated by the addition of a Z (*zwerg*), meaning "dwarf," to indicate miniature Dachshunds.

AMERICAN POPULARITY

In America, Dachshunds have not been used for hunting ground game such as badger and wild boar, nor for tracking wounded deer. The dogs' lively character, courage and devotion have always made them very popular, nonetheless. Dachshunds were imported to America well before the American Kennel Club initiated its stud book in 1885.

By 1895, the Dachshund Club of America advanced the breed's popularity by promoting the hunting aspects of the dogs through badger-dog hunting trials. In 1913, Dachs-

Dachsies are very popular among owners today because of the breed's devotion and courage.

True Tails

Meet two Dachshunds. Both are loved by their families and both are happy dogs, yet they have very different lifestyles.

Whiskers is a one-year-old neutered male. He's a longhaired standard, black and tan in color. By nature he's a quiet dog who loves children and family friends. He's typically "Dachshund stubborn," yet is teachable because he enjoys learning new things and doing things with his owners. Whiskers gets along well with other dogs and particularly loves a four-year-old female mixed-breed who shares his home. He also does well with other household pets, such as two cats and two hamsters. When asked what's the best thing about Whiskers, his owners quickly respond, "He's very mellow—like us!"

Now meet Tootsie, a smooth miniature, red in color, who was deserted by her owners when she was three-and-a-half years old. Fortunately for Tootsie, she was rescued by a woman who enjoyed dog obedience competition and had always wanted to own a Dachshund. Tootsie began obedience training and soon amassed a list of obedience wins that would impress even the toughest judge. Then she began agility training and fell in love with the sport. Today, at ten years of age, Tootsie has earned four agility titles

in two organizations. The list of Tootsie's accomplishments is almost bigger than she is! At home, Tootsie sleeps in her owner's bed under the covers (a place familiar to many Dachsies). She loves having guests visit her home and is an excellent ambassador for all Dachshunds.

Despite the differences in lifestyle between Whiskers and Tootsie, both dogs are well-adjusted and cherished members of their families. These two dogs serve as examples of how versatile the Dachshund can be as he makes his life with humans and brings his owners great pleasure and comfort.

hunds were listed among the 10 most popular breeds in America. When World War I began, the interest in Dachshunds declined and remained low until the early 1930s. By 1940, they were again ranked among the top ten breeds in America and maintained that rank well into the 21st century.

In Germany, miniature Dachshunds are shown in a special class for dogs weighing less than 9 pounds; however, this is not the case in the United States. In America, standard and miniature Dachshunds (of the same coat variety) compete in the same class, with dogs weighing 11 pounds or less than at twelve months of age being shown in a special division.

WORLDWIDE WIENERS

England established a Dachshund specialty club even before one was begun in

Did You Know?

In Germany, Dachshunds are measured by the size of the hole that the dog can enter in pursuit of game, as opposed to pounds or inches like most other breeds.
The German divide the breed into three categories. The standard Dachsie is known as Normalgrossteckel, while the miniature Dachsie is divided into two categories Zwertgteckel (which means "dwarf" and measures 13.8 inches around the chest) and Kaninchenteckel (which means "rabbit" and measures 11.8 inches).

There's no better breed to snuggle up and cuddle with than a Dachshund!

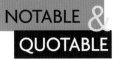 NOTABLE & QUOTABLE

During World War I, there was much disdain over anything considered German, and unfortunately, the Dachshund was a victim of much hostility. They were sometimes the victims of stonings, and Dachshund owners were often called traitors.

—Ann Gordon of Pittsburgh, Pa., a Dachshund judge

Germany. Indeed, despite the tensions triggered by World War I, England claimed six noted Dachshund breeders who adhered to a strict breeding code throughout the war. Though these breeders were often referred to as "pro-German" or "German sympathizers," they held firm to the integrity of the Dachshund in order to preserve its genetic foundation. Moreover, their efforts to protect the early gene pool succeeded.

Two of the earliest English Dachshunds to leave an indelible mark on the breed in the 1890s were Jackdaw, owned by Harry Jones of Ipswich, and Pterodactyl, owned by Sidney Woodiwiss. Those early ancestors still influence the breed today.

Australia, Denmark, Holland, and India are also countries where Dachshunds are popular. In the United Kingdom, the miniature longhaired Dachshund is the favorite hound breed, outnumbering even British

Dachshunds have been popular in the show-dog world (upper right) and with artists (upper left and lower left) for centuries.

hounds like the Basset Hound, Beagle, and Whippet, the latter being the second most popular breed.

The Dachshund's versatile nature makes him a popular breed to own and love.

MODERN-DAY DACHSIES

Today, the Dachshund has come full circle. The breed is once more appreciated for its original purpose—hunting and "going to ground." More and more Dachshund owners are testing their dogs' abilities in the field, becoming active in performance events, such as earthdog tests and field trials, as well as agility (with its tunnels seemingly made for Dachshunds) and obedience.

When he's not busy showing off his stuff, the Dachshund makes a wonderful lap or bed dog, admirers say.

Why has the Dachshund's popularity endured? The breed's appeal is in its diversity, versatility, and adaptability. The fact that Dachshunds come in two sizes (standard and miniature) and three coat types is simply the relish on the hot dog. What more could one ask for?

it's a Fact

Queen Victoria's husband, the German Prince Albert, brought Dachshunds to England in 1839, and presented one to his new wife—a dog that she named Dash. The royal couple buried one of their Dachshunds at Windsor Castle. His monument consists of a solid pillar that stands about 6 feet high. On it is inscribed: "Here is buried Deckel, the faithful German Dachshund of Queen Victoria, who brought him from Cobug in 1845. Died August 10, 1859, aged 15 years."

So you've decided that you can't live much longer without a Dachshund of your own. Few breeds have the appeal and uniqueness of the Dachshund, in all his many forms and colors.

If you've decided upon which size and coat variety you prefer, it's time to figure out where to find the right puppy. Inquire about breeders in your area who have a good reputation; many breeders specialize in one coat type and size, while others dabble in a few. You are looking for an established breeder, someone who's been breeding Dachshunds for at least ten years and who belongs to his local and national breed clubs. Such a breeder has demonstrated outstanding dog ethics and a strong commitment to the breed. An established breeder will be happy to answer your questions and make you comfortable with your choice of the Dachshund, even being able to explain the subtle differences in temperament and behavior between the varieties.

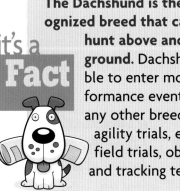

it's a Fact

The Dachshund is the only AKC-recognized breed that can and does hunt above and below ground. Dachshunds are eligible to enter more AKC performance events than almost any other breed, including agility trials, earthdog tests, field trials, obedience trials, and tracking tests.

Finding a healthy puppy starts with finding a quality breeder.

A good Dachshund breeder will sell you a puppy at a fair price if, and only if, he determines that you would be a suitable, worthy owner for his dogs. A responsible breeder can be relied upon for advice, no matter what time of day or night, and will accept a puppy back, without questions, should you decide that this is not the right dog for you.

When choosing a breeder, reputation and qualifications are much more important than where the breeder is located. A three- or four-hour drive to pick up a new family member should not be considered an inconvenience.

Choosing a breeder is an important first step in dog ownership. Fortunately, most Dachshund breeders are devoted to the breed and its well-being, though be aware

A Dachshund owner should be willing to explain things to the dog. I know this sounds weird, but a Dachsie will do almost anything for you as long as the dog understands it. If he thinks you're wasting his time, he will ignore you.—Dachshund fancier Charlee Helms of Midland, Texas

that there are backyard Dachsie "breeders" who take advantage of the breed's popularity and the ignorance of many new dog purchasers. With a little research and knowledge, smart owners should have little problem finding a reputable breeder who doesn't live too far away. Start with your local all-breed kennel club or Dachshund club. The American Kennel Club can direct you to the club or clubs nearest you; visit them online at www.akc.org. The Dachshund Club of America maintains a breeder–referral service and also can put you in touch with your local club. The DCA can be found online at www.dachshund–dca.org.

Referrals are an excellent way to find a puppy. If you see a Dachshund you like, find out where he came from. Ask about health problems and temperament, and ask if the breeder was pleasant to work with. If that breeder doesn't have a puppy for you, he may be able to refer you to someone with similar lines.

Potential owners are encouraged to attend dog shows, obedience trails, or other kinds of performance events to see Dachshunds in action, to meet the owners and handlers firsthand, and to get an idea of what Dachshunds look like outside a photographer's lens. New owners may be surprised to see how large a standard Dachshund male is, or

Ask to meet the mother and father of the pups, if possible. They will give you a clue into what your future puppy will look and act like.

how small a miniature Dachshund female is. There's nothing like seeing Dachsies live and up close. Provided you approach the handlers or owners at dog shows when they are not terribly busy, most are more than willing to answer questions, recommend breeders and give advice. Dachsie people love to talk about their favorite topic: wieners!

MEET AND GREET

Now it's time to meet one or two breeders and their dogs. If the breeder has young puppies, he may not allow you to visit for a few weeks to ensure their safety. Whether he has puppies when you visit or not, never go from one kennel to another without going home, showering and changing clothes, including your shoes (or clean them thoroughly, and spray the bottoms and sides with a ten–percent bleach solution). It is extremely easy to transmit deadly infectious

Did You Know? **Signs of a Good Breeder** When you visit a breeder, be on the lookout for:
- a clean, well-maintained facility
- no overwhelming odors
- overall impression of cleanliness
- socialized dogs and puppies

disease and parasites from one kennel to another, even if everything looks clean.

Meet as many of your potential puppy's relatives as possible. You should be able to meet the mother unless the puppies are very young. Don't expect her to look her best while she's nursing—puppy care is a big job for canine moms. Pay attention to her temperament. It is normal for a female dog to be protective of her babies, but she should accept your presence if her owner vouches for you. If the sire (father) is on the property, ask to meet him. He may not be present, because serious breeders often breed their bitches to stud dogs owned by other people. You should be able to see pictures of him, though. If you don't like the

Did You Know?

Dachshunds who weigh between 11 and 16 pounds (between the miniature and standard weight classes) are affectionately known as "tweenies."

parents—either the body type or temperament—don't buy the puppy. Pups tend to look and act like their parents.

Take a look around. Does the environment look and smell reasonably clean? Do all the dogs appear to be healthy, with clear eyes, trimmed nails and well-groomed coats? Do they have fresh water to drink and room to move and play? Are they friendly? Does the breeder know every dog by name and each puppy as an individual? If the answer to any of these questions is "no," look elsewhere. If the answers are "yes," though, and you feel comfortable with this breeder and like his dogs, and he feels comfortable with you, you may soon be owned by a Dachshund puppy!

SELECTING A PUPPY

Once you have contacted and met a breeder or two and made your choice about which breeder is best suited to your needs,

it's time to visit the litter. Keep in mind that many top breeders have waiting lists. Sometimes new owners have to wait as long as two years for a puppy. If you are really committed to the breeder you've selected, then you will wait (and hope for an early arrival!). If not, you may have to resort to your second- or third-choice breeder. Don't be too anxious, however. If the breeder doesn't have anyone interested in his puppies, there is probably a good reason.

Because breeding the Dachshund is a very delicate matter, and breeders must always test their breeding stock before producing a litter, most breeders do not expect a litter every season, or, for that matter, even every year. Patience is a true Dachshund virtue.

You are likely choosing a Dachshund as a pet dog and not as a show or hunting dog, so select a pup who is friendly and attractive. Dachshunds generally have relatively

---

JOIN OUR ONLINE Dachsie Club

Q&A for Owners
Be prepared for the breeder to ask you some questions.

1. Have you previously owned a Dachshund?
The breeder is trying to gauge how familiar you are with the breed. If you have never owned one, illustrate your knowledge of Dachshunds by telling the breeder about your research.

2. Do you have children? How old are they?
Some breeders are wary about selling a small dog to families with younger children. This isn't a steadfast rule, and some breeders only insist on meeting the children first to see how they handle puppies. It all depends on the breeder.

3. How long have you wanted a Dachshund?
This helps a breeder know if this purchase is an impulse buy, or a carefully thought-out decision. Buying on impulse is one of the biggest mistakes owners can make. Getting a Dachshund puppy is not as quick as downloading the latest iTunes song. Be patient. It may take a week to find the right dog, or even a year. It really depends on timing. Join Club Dachsie to get a complete list of questions a breeder should ask you. Click on "downloads" at **DogChannel.com/Club-Dachsie**

Choose a pup with traits that mesh well with you and your family, not just one with a color or coat style you like.

small litters, averaging five puppies, so selection is limited once you have located a desirable breeder. Beware of the shy or overly aggressive puppy; be especially conscious of the nervous Dachshund pup. Don't let sentiment or emotion trap you into buying the runt of the litter.

Try to divorce yourself from preconceived color preferences. Once you've found a healthy, socialized litter from a responsible, reputable breeder, in the size and coat variety of your choice, you do not want to struggle with color disappointment. Finding a dappled longhaired puppy or a chocolate

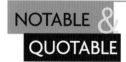

Are you looking for a pet who will worship the ground you walk on?

Rescue volunteers suggest that people peel their eyes away from those appealing, tempting puppies and consider adopting an older Dachshund who's four, five, or six years old—or even older.

Sometimes, a Dachshund finds himself without a home. Perhaps the owner decides he can't or won't put in the time needed to care for the dog or can't figure out how to train him. Such a dog may be surrendered to a Dachshund rescue group, which then works to find him a permanent home.

These groups sometimes have young puppies available for adoption, and often have older puppies or adolescents. To find a Dachshund rescue group, log onto the Dachshund Club of America's website at: www.dachshund-dca.org

There are plenty of benefits to adopting a rescued Dachsie. Such dogs have passed the chewing stage, have learned basic bathroom manners—and still have many years left. In addition, many rescue volunteers believe that the older dog realizes he's been saved, and repays his savior by showing lots of love and devotion.

Another way to find a Dachshund puppy who needs a new home is to log onto a national pet adoption website such as Petfinder.com (www.petfinder.com). The site's searchable database enables you to find a Dachsie puppy in your area who needs a break in the form of a compassionate owner like you.

and fawn wirehaired puppy will be far more difficult than simply locating a quality long-haired or wirehaired puppy. All Dachshund colors and color combinations are attractive, so keep health and sound breeding foremost in your selection and worry about color last.

Breeders allow visitors to see the litter by around the fifth or sixth week, and puppies leave for their new homes at eight to ten weeks of age. Breeders who sell their puppies earlier are more interested in money than in their puppies' well-being. Puppies need to learn from their mothers, and most moms continue teaching manners and dos and don'ts until around the eighth week.

Breeders spend significant amounts of time with the Dachshund toddlers so that the pups are able to interact with humans. Given the long history that dogs and humans have, bonding between the two species is natural but must be nurtured. A well-bred, well-socialized Dachshund pup wants nothing more than to be near you and to please you.

ESSENTIAL PAPERWORK

Make sure the breeder has proper papers to go with the puppy of your choice.

Contract: You should receive a copy of the purchase contract you signed when you bought your puppy. The contract should specify the purchase price, health guarantee, spay/neuter requirements by a certain age, and conditions to return the pup if you find you can't keep her for any reason.

Registration Papers: If the breeder said that the puppy's parents were registered

---

Breeder Q&A

Here are some questions you should ask a breeder and the preferred answers you want.

Q: What types of Dachshunds do you raise?
A: There is no right or wrong answer. You just want to make sure the breeder has the kind of Dachsie you want.

Q. How often do you have litters available?
A. The answer you want to hear is "once or twice a year" or "occasionally" because a breeder who doesn't have litters all that often is probably more concerned with the quality of his puppies, rather than with producing a lot of puppies to make money.

Q. What is the goal of your breeding program?
A. A good answer is "to improve the breed" or "to breed for temperament."

Q. What kinds of health problems have you had with your Dachshunds?
A. Beware of a breeder who says, "none." Every breed has health issues. For Dachsies, some problems include spinal troubles, epilepsy, eye problems, elbow dysplasia (the elbow joint doesn't fit together) and patellar luxation (dislocated kneecaps).

Get a complete list of questions to ask a Dachshund breed—and the correct answers—on Club Dachsie. Log onto **DogChannel.com/Club-Dachsie** and click on "downloads."

Most times, it's best to let the breeder choose the right puppy for you. He is more familiar with the pups, and is more likely to make the perfect match.

Did You Know?

If you purchase a Dachshund who is not eligible for American Kennel Club registration, your dog may still be able to participate in companion and performance events. The Purebred Alternative Listing Program/Indefinite Listing Privilege allows unregistered Dachsies to enter agility trials, earthdog trials, junior showmanship at dog shows, and obedience and rally trials. Visit the **AKC's** website for an application (**www.akc.org**).

with the American Kennel Club or United Kennel Club, you should receive an application form to register your puppy—or at the very least, a signed bill of sale that you can use to register the puppy. The bill of sale should include the puppy's breed, date of birth, sex, registered names of the parents, litter number, the breeder's name, date of sale, and the seller's signature. Registration allows your puppy to compete in kennel club-sanctioned events such as agility, obedience and earthdog trials. Registration fees support research and other activities sponsored by the organization. If your intention is to show your Dachshund, be sure not to purchase a puppy that the breeder promises is "AKC registration eligible" because it's unlikely he will be; only fully registered dogs can participate in AKC conformation shows.

Pedigree: The breeder should include a copy of your puppy's family tree, listing your puppy's parents, grandparents, great-grandparents, and beyond, depending on how many generations the pedigree includes. It also lists any degrees and/or

The Dachshund was developed to help hunters in situations where the traditional hunting breeds were too large. The Dachsie has been prized for his hunting skills, and has been owned by royalty and commoners alike.

titles that those relatives have earned. Look for indications that the dog's ancestors were active and successful achievers in various dog sports. The information that a pedigree provides can help you understand more about the physical conformation and/or behavioral accomplishments of your puppy's family. Usually the quality of the pedigree dictates the price of the puppy, so expect to pay a higher price for a higher quality puppy. However, chances are that you will be rewarded by the quality of life that you and your pedigreed puppy will enjoy!

Health Records: You should receive a copy of your puppy's health records, including his date of birth, visits to the veterinarian and immunizations. Bring the health records to your veterinarian when you take your puppy in for his first checkup, which should take place within a few days of his arrival in your household. The records will become part of your puppy's permanent health file.

Care Instructions: Finally, a responsible Dachshund breeder will provide each new owner with written instructions on basic puppy care, including when and how much to feed their new Dachsie.

Among other papers, the breeder should send you home with info on how to properly care for your precious pooch.

Signs of a Healthy Puppy

Here are a few things you should look for when selecting a puppy from a litter.

1. **NOSE:** It should be slightly moist to the touch, but there shouldn't be excessive discharge. The puppy should not be sneezing or sniffling persistently.

2. **SKIN AND COAT:** The puppy's coat should be soft and shiny, without flakes or excessive shedding. Watch out for patches of missing hair, redness, bumps, or sores. The pup should have a pleasant smell. Check for parasites, such as fleas or ticks.

3. **BEHAVIOR:** A healthy puppy may be sleepy, but should not be lethargic. A healthy pup will be playful at times, not isolated in a corner. You should see occasional bursts of energy and interaction with littermates. When it's mealtime, a healthy pup will take an interest in his food.

There are more signs to look for when picking out the perfect Dachshund puppy. Download the list at **DogChannel.com/Club-Dachsie**

Most puppies are only pet-quality, meaning they are not able to be shown in dog shows. That doesn't mean they're inferior; they still make great pets!

Researching the breed and finding a breeder are only two aspects of the homework a smart owner will have to do before bringing home a Dachshund puppy. You also will have to prepare your home and family for the new addition. Much as you would prepare a nursery for a newborn baby, you will need to designate a place in your home that will be the puppy's own.

How you prepare your home will depend on how much freedom the dog will be allowed. In the case of your Dachshund, designating a couple of rooms (without stairs) for the puppy is ideal. Dachshund puppies should not be permitted to jump up on furniture or maneuver stairs because both activities can injure the puppy's long, fragile back. These activities should be forbidden from the very beginning so that your puppy understands that he belongs "low to the ground" as he was created!

In order for a puppy to grow into a stable, well-adjusted dog, he has to feel comfortable in his surroundings. Remember, he is leaving the warmth and security of his

Did You Know?

Oftentimes, Dachsies become especially attached to one member of the family. The choice is usually based on which person they spend the most time with. Some dogs attach themselves to only one person in a family while ignoring the other members. This situation can be avoided if the entire family participates in activities with the dog as well as practices obedience exercises with him. The dog must learn that he is part of the whole family, not just one isolated member.

mother and littermates, as well as the familiarity of the only place he has ever known, so it is important to make his transition to your home—his new home—as easy as possible.

PUPPY-PROOFING

Aside from making sure that your Dachshund will be comfortable in your home, you also have to make sure that your home is safe, which means taking the proper precautions to keep your pup away from things that are dangerous for him.

Puppy-proof your home inside and out. Place breakables out of reach. If he is limited to certain places within the house, keep potentially dangerous items in "off-limit" areas. If your Dachshund is going to spend time in a crate, make sure that there is nothing near his crate that he can reach if he sticks his curious little nose or paws through the openings.

The outside of your home must also be safe for your pup. Your Dachsie will naturally want to run and explore the yard, and he should be granted that freedom—as long as you are there to supervise him. Do not let a fence give you a false sense of security; you will be surprised by how crafty (and persistent) a dog can be in figuring out how to dig under a fence or squeeze through small holes. The remedy is to make the fence well embedded into the ground, keeping in mind that Dachshunds are diggers, who were bred to go through small holes. Any Dachsie person knows that his dog can burrow with remarkable skill and speed. Be sure to repair or secure any gaps in the fence. Check the fence periodically to

SMART TIP!

A well-stocked toy box should contain three main categories of toys:
1. **action** (anything that you can throw or roll and get things moving)
2. **distraction** (durable toys that make dogs work for a treat)
3. **comfort** (soft, stuffed little "security blankets")

ensure that it is in good shape and make repairs as needed; a very determined pup may work on the same spot until he is able to get through.

The following are a few common problem areas to watch out for in the home.

Electrical cords and wiring: No electrical cord or wiring is safe. Office-supply stores sell products to keep wires gathered under computer desks, as well as products

When puppy-proofing your house, also check the yard for any potential dangers.

Be aware of sprays in your yard, as these poisons could end up in your dog's body.

lock if necessary. Be aware that dogs love bathroom trash (i.e., cotton balls, cotton swabs, used razors, dental floss, etc.), which consists of items that are all extremely dangerous! Put this trash can in a cabinet under the sink and make sure you always shut the door to the bathroom.

Household cleaners: Make sure that your puppy doesn't have access to any of these deadly chemicals. Keep them behind closed cabinet doors, using child-safe locks if necessary.

Pest-control sprays and other poisons: Chemicals to control ants or other pests should never be used in the house, if possible. Your puppy doesn't have to directly ingest these poisons to become ill; if he steps in the poison, he can experience toxic effects by licking his paws. Roach

that prevent office chair wheels (and puppy teeth) from damaging electrical cords. If you have exposed cords and wires, these products aren't very expensive and can be used to keep a pup out of trouble.

Trash cans: Don't waste your time trying to "train" your Dachsie not to get into the trash. Simply put the trash or garbage behind a cabinet door and use a child-safe

motels and other poisonous pest traps are also evidently yummy to dogs, so don't drop these behind couches or cabinets; it's quite possible that if there's room for a motel, there's room for a determined Dachshund.

Fabric: Here's one you might not think about: Some Dachsie puppies have a habit of licking blankets, upholstery, rugs, or carpets. Though this habit seems fairly innocu-

The first thing you should always do before your puppy comes home is to lie on the ground and look around. You want to be able to see everything your puppy is going to see. For the puppy, the world is one big chew toy.

—Cathleen Stamm, founder of 2nd Chance Dachshund Rescue in San Diego, Calif.

ous, over time the fibers from the upholstery or carpet can accumulate in the dog's stomach and cause a blockage. If you see your dog licking any of these items, remove the item or prevent your Dachsie from having contact with it.

Prescriptions, painkillers, supplements and vitamins: Keeping medications on a counter or the kitchen table isn't safe. All medications should be kept in a high cabinet. Also, be very careful when taking your prescription medications, supplements or vitamins: How often have you dropped a pill? With a Dachshund, you can be assured that your puppy will be in between your legs and will snarf up the

SMART TIP!

9-1-1! If you don't know whether the plant or food or "stuff" your Dachshund just ate is toxic to dogs, call the ASPCA's Animal Poison Control Center (888-426-4435). Be prepared to provide your puppy's age and weight, his symptoms—if any—and how much of the plant, chemical, or substance he ingested, as well as how long ago you think he came into contact with the substance. The ASPCA charges a consultation fee for this service.

Many outdoor plants are harmful to dogs if eaten in sufficient amounts. If you're not sure if what your dog ate is OK, contact a poison control center ASAP.

Keeping your Dachsie safe should be a priority.

pill before you can even start to say "No!" Dispense your own pills carefully and without your Dachsie present.

Miscellaneous loose items: If it's not bolted to the floor, your Dachsie is likely to give the item a taste test. Socks, coins, children's toys, game pieces, cat bell balls—you name it; if it's on the floor, it's worth a try. Make sure the floors in your home are picked up and free of clutter.

FAMILY INTRODUCTIONS

Everyone in the house will be excited about your puppy's homecoming and will want to pet him and play with him, but it is best to make the introduction low-key so as not to overwhelm the puppy. He is apprehensive already. It is the first time he has been separated from his mother, littermates, and the breeder; the ride to your home is likely to be the first time he has been in a car. The last thing you want to do is smother your Dachshund, as this will only frighten him further. This is not to say that human contact is not extremely necessary at this stage, because this is the time when a connection between the pup and his human family is formed. Gentle petting and soothing words should help console your Dachshund, as well as just putting him down and letting him explore on his own (under your watchful eye, of course).

Your pup may approach family members or may busy himself with exploring for a while. Gradually, each person should spend some time with the pup, one at a time, crouching

down to get as close to the Dachshund's level as possible and letting him sniff their hands before petting him gently. He definitely needs human attention and he needs to be touched; this is how to form an immediate bond. Just remember that the puppy is experiencing a lot of things for the first time, at the same time. There are new people, new noises, new smells, and new things to investigate, so be gentle, be affectionate, and be as comforting as you can be.

PUP'S FIRST NIGHT HOME

You have traveled home with your new Dachsie safely in his crate. He may have already been to the vet for a thorough check-up, he's been weighed, his papers examined; perhaps he's even been vaccinated and dewormed as well. Your Dachshund has met and licked the whole family, including the excited children and the less-than-happy cat. He's explored his area, his new bed, the yard and anywhere else he's permitted. He's eaten his first meal at home and relieved himself in the proper place. Your Dachshund has heard lots of new sounds, smelled new friends and seen more of

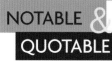

NOTABLE & QUOTABLE

Playing with toys from puppyhood encourages good behavior and social skills. A happy, playful dog is a content and well-adjusted one. Also, because all puppies chew to soothe their gums and help loosen puppy teeth, they should always have easy access to several different toys.

— *dog trainer Harrison Forbes of Savannah, Tenn.*

the outside world than ever before.

This was just the first day! He's worn out and is ready for bed—or so you think! Remember, this is your puppy's first night sleeping alone. His mother and littermates are no longer at paw's length, and he's scared, cold, and lonely. Be reassuring to your new family member, but don't spoil your Dachshund and give in to his inevitable whining.

Puppies whine to let others know where they are and hopefully to get company out of it. Place your pup in his new bed or crate and close the door. Mercifully, he may fall asleep without a peep. If the inevitable occurs, ignore the whining; he is fine. Do not give in and visit the pup. He will fall asleep eventually.

Many breeders recommend placing a piece of bedding from his former home in

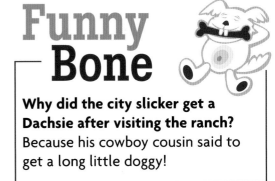

Funny Bone

Why did the city slicker get a Dachsie after visiting the ranch? Because his cowboy cousin said to get a long little doggy!

his new bed so that he recognizes the scent of his littermates. Others still advise placing a hot water bottle in his bed for warmth. The latter may be a good idea provided the pup doesn't attempt to suckle; he'll get good and wet and may not fall asleep so fast.

Your Dachshund's first night can be somewhat stressful for him and you!

Introduce your pup to new people and things slowly so he doesn't become overwhelmed.

Any Dachsie home should include lots of toys and fun stuff to play with.

Remember that you are setting the tone of nighttime at your house. Unless you want to play with your pup every night at 10 p.m., midnight and 2 a.m., don't initiate the habit. Your family will thank you, and so will your pup!

SHOPPING FOR A DACHSHUND

It's fun shopping for a new puppy. From training to feeding and sleeping to playing, your new Dachshund will need a few items to make life comfy, easy, and fun. Be prepared and visit your local pet-supply store before you bring home your new family member.

Collar and ID tag: Accustom your dog to wearing a collar the first day you bring him home. Not only will a collar and ID tag help your pup in the event that he becomes lost, but collars are also an important training tool. If your Dachsie gets into trouble, the collar will act as a handle, helping you divert him to a more appropriate behavior. Make sure the collar fits snugly enough so that your Dachsie cannot wriggle out of it, but is

SMART TIP!

When teaching a Dachshund to accept and like children, be sure that the children move slowly rather than with erratic, fast motions. Dachshunds see fast-moving things as prey and will go after them, even though these "things" may be children. Once the dog becomes accustomed to children, he will accept the running and playing of his young human friends.

loose enough so that it will not be uncomfortably tight around his neck. You should be able to fit a finger between the pup and the collar. Collars come in many styles, but for starting out, a simple buckle collar with an easy-release snap works great.

Leash: For training or just for taking a stroll, a leash is your Dachsie's vehicle to explore the outside world. Like collars, leashes come in a variety of styles and materials. A 6-foot nylon leash is a popular

choice because they are lightweight and durable. As your pup grows and gets used to walking on the leash, you may want to purchase a flexible leash. These leads allow you to extend the length to give the dog a broader area to explore or to shorten the length to keep the dog closer to you. Of course, there are special leashes for training purposes, and specially made harnesses for working dogs, but these are not necessary for routine walks.

Bowls: Your Dachshund will need two bowls: one for water and one for food. You may want two sets of bowls, one for inside and one for outside, depending on where the dog will be fed and where she will be spending time. Bowls should be sturdy enough so that they don't tip over easily. (Most have reinforced bottoms that prevent tipping.) Bowls are made of metal, ceramic, or plastic. Make sure yours are easy to clean.

Crate: A crate is multipurpose. It serves as a bed, house-training tool and travel carrier. It also is the ideal doggie den—a bedroom of sorts—that your Dachshund can retire to when she wants to rest or just needs a break. The crate should be large enough for your Dachshund to stand in, turn around, and lie down. You don't want any more room than this—especially if you're planning on using the crate to house-train your dog—because he will eliminate in one corner and lie down

Den-lovers at heart, Dachsies take especially well to crates.

in another. Get a crate that is big enough for your dog when she is an adult. Use dividers to limit the space when he's a puppy.

Bed: A plush doggie bed will make sleeping and resting more comfortable for your Dachsie. Dog beds come in all shapes, sizes and colors, but your dog just needs one that is soft and large enough for him to stretch out on. Because puppies and rescue dogs often don't come house-trained, it's helpful to buy a bed that can be washed easily. If your Dachsie will be sleeping in a crate, a nice crate pad and a small blanket that he can "burrow" in will help him feel more at home. Replace the blanket if it becomes ragged and starts to fall apart because your Dachsie's nails could get caught in it.

Gate: Similar to those used for toddlers, gates help keep your Dachshund confined to one room or area when you can't supervise him. Gates also work to keep your dog out of areas you don't want him in. Gates are available in many styles. For Dachsies, make sure the one you choose has openings small enough so your wiener dog can't squeeze through the bars or openings on the gate.

Toys: Keep your dog occupied and entertained by providing him with an array of fun toys. Teething puppies like to chew—in fact, chewing is a physical need for pups as they are teething—and everything from your shoes to the leather couch to the Oriental rug is fair game. Divert your Dachsie's chewing instincts with durable toys like bones made of nylon or hard rubber. Other fun toys include rope toys, treat-dispensing toys and balls. Make sure the toys and bones don't have any small parts that could break off and be swallowed, causing your dog to choke. Stuffed toys are popular, but they can become destuffed, and an overly excited puppy may ingest the stuffing or the squeaker. Check your Dachsie's toys regularly and replace them if they

it's a Fact

Dachshunds were originally bred to seek out prey. Keep that in mind when puppy-proofing your home.

If you're not sure where to get the essentials for your Dachsie, ask a store clerk at a pet-supply store for help.

become frayed or show signs of wear.

Cleaning supplies: Until your Dachsie pup is house-trained, you will be doing a lot of cleaning. Accidents will occur, which is acceptable in the beginning because the puppy does not know any better. All you can do is be prepared to clean them up. Old rags, towels, newspapers, and a stain and odor remover are good to have on hand.

BEYOND THE BASICS

The items previously discussed are the bare necessities. You will find out what else you need as you go along—grooming supplies, flea/tick protection, etc. These things will vary depending on your situation, but it is important that you have everything you need to make your Dachshund comfortable during his first few days at home.

Some ordinary household items make great toys for your Dachshund—as long you make sure they are safe. You will find a list of homemade toys at **DogChannel.com/Club-Dachsie**

HOUSE-TRAINING

Dachshunds are notorious for being difficult to house-train. In fact, lots of small dogs seem to offer this challenge. There are several reasons for this: It's easier to miss a small dog's "I gotta go" signals; smaller dog, smaller mess; messes are easier to miss; etc. It also may be true that because a small dog's organs are smaller, they don't have the capacity to hold it for as long as a big dog.

In any case, the answer to successful house-training is total supervision and management—crates, tethers, exercise pens, and leashes—until you know your dog has developed substrate preferences for outside surfaces (grass, gravel, concrete) instead of carpet, tile, or hardwood, and knows that potty happens outside.

IN THE BEGINNING

For the first two to three weeks of a puppy's life, his mother helps him to eliminate. The mother also keeps the whelping box or "nest area" clean. When pups begin to walk around and eat on their own, they

it's a **Fact**

Ongoing house-training difficulties may indicate your puppy has a health problem, warranting a veterinary checkup. A urinary infection, parasites, a virus, and other nasty issues greatly affect your puppy's ability to hold pee or poop.

choose where they eliminate. You can train your puppy to relieve himself wherever you choose, but this must be somewhere suitable. You should bear in mind from the outset that when your Dachshund is old enough to go out in public places, any canine deposits must be removed at once. You will always have to carry a small plastic bag or "poop-scoop" with you.

Smart owners must first decide on which surface and location they want their Dachshund puppy to use. Make sure it is going to be permanent. Training your dog to eliminate on grass and changing two months later is extremely difficult for the dog.

Next, choose the command that you will use each and every time you want your puppy to void. "Let's go," "hurry up," and "potty" are examples of cues commonly used by dog owners.

Get in the habit of giving your Dachsie the relief command before you take him out. That way, when he becomes an adult, you will be able to determine if he wants to go out when you ask him. A confirmation will be signs of interest, such as wagging his tail, watching you intently, going to the door, etc.

LET'S START WITH THE CRATE

Clean animals by nature, dogs keenly dislike soiling where they sleep and eat. This fact makes a crate a useful tool for house-training. When purchasing a new crate, consider that one correctly sized will allow adequate room for an adult dog to stand full-height, lie on his side without scrunching and turn around easily. If debating plastic versus wire crates, shorthaired breeds sometimes prefer the warmer, draft-blocking quality of plastic, while furry dogs often like the cooling airflow of a wire crate.

Some crates come equipped with a movable wall that reduces the interior size to provide enough space for your Dachsie to stand, turn and lie down, while not allowing room to soil one end and sleep in the other. The problem is that if your puppy goes potty in the crate anyway, the divider forces him to lie in his own excrement.

This can work against you by desensitizing your puppy against his normal, instinctive revulsion to resting where he's eliminated. If scheduling permits you or a responsible family member to clean the crate soon after it's soiled, you can still crate-train because limiting crate size does encourage your puppy to hold it. Otherwise, give him enough room to move away

Teaching this biddable breed to potty outside should be a breeze, as they are usually eager learners.

from an unclean area until he's better able to control his elimination.

Needless to say, not every puppy adheres to this guideline. If your Dachshund moves along at a faster pace, thank your lucky stars. Should he progress slower, accept it and remind yourself that he'll improve. Be aware that pups frequently hold it longer at night than during the day. Just because your puppy sleeps for six or more hours through the night, does not mean he can hold it that long during the more active daytime hours.

One last bit of advice on the crate: Place it in the corner of a normally trafficked room, such as the family room or kitchen. Social and curious by nature, dogs like to feel included in family happenings. Creating a

quiet retreat by putting the crate in an unused area may seem like a good idea, but results in your Dachsie feeling insecure and isolated. Watching his people pop in and out of the crate room reassures your puppy that he's not forgotten.

A PUPPY'S NEEDS

Your puppy needs to relieve himself after play periods, after each meal, after he has been sleeping and any time he indicates that he is looking for a place to potty.

The urinary and intestinal tract muscles of very young puppies are not fully developed. Therefore, puppies need to relieve themselves frequently. Take your Dachsie out often—every hour for an 8-week-old, for example—and

True Tails

Jeremy Campbell of Costa Mesa, Calif., has found a devoted companion in his Dachshund, Jackson. "He's amazing," Campbell says of his mini. "We do everything together."

Never having owned a dog before, Campbell fell for the chocolate Dachsie, who was the only dog in the kennel not biting the other dogs or clamoring to get out. "He seemed to be so mellow," Campbell says. But any new puppy owner will tell you that low-key is the last thing you can expect from your dog, and to this day, Campbell is still learning how to live harmoniously with his furry fireball.

Although his puppy stage included the usual endless energy and nonstop chewing, Jackson contradicted most Dachshund stereotypes. Although it is typically an obstacle for new owners of any breed of puppy, house-training came easily to this little guy.

"He sort of trained me," Campbell admits. "He got really good very early on at letting me know when he needed to go." During Jackson's first checkup, the vet explained that Campbell would probably be the one who needed training. "And it's turned out just like that. I've tried to follow his advice, and it's worked."

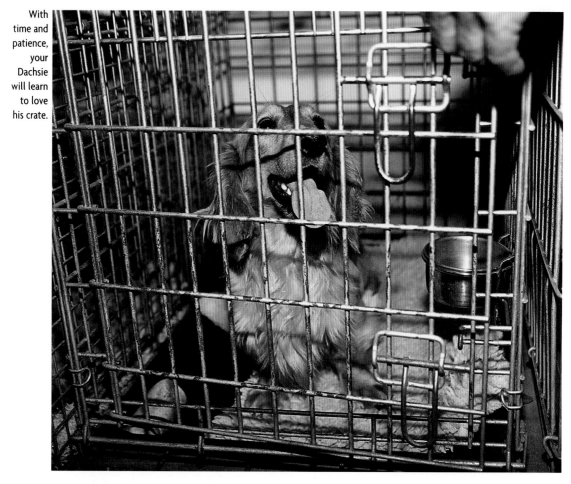

immediately after a nap and eating. The older the puppy, the less often he will need to relieve himself. Finally, as a mature, healthy adult, he will require only three to five relief trips per day.

HOUSING HELPS

Because the types of housing and control you provide for your puppy have a direct relationship on the success of house-training, consider the various aspects of both before beginning training.

Taking a new puppy home and turning him loose in your house can be compared to turning a child loose in a sports arena and telling the child that the place is all his! The sheer enormity of the place would be too much to handle.

NOTABLE & QUOTABLE *Reward your pup with a high-value treat immediately after he potties to reinforce going in the proper location, then play for a short time afterward. This teaches that good things happen after pottying outside!*—Victoria Schade, certified pet dog trainer, from Annandale, Va.

Pick a potty spot for your pup that is out of the way, but not so far that he has to walk a long way to get there.

Instead, offer your Dachsie clearly defined areas where he can play, sleep, eat, and live. A room of the house where the family gathers is the most obvious choice. Puppies are social

SMART TIP!

When proximity prevents you from going home at lunch or during periods when overtime crops up, make alternative arrangements for getting your puppy out. Hire a pet sitting or walking service, or enlist the aid of an obliging neighbor willing to help.

animals and need to feel a part of the pack right from the start. Hearing your voice, watching you while you are doing things and smelling you nearby are all positive reinforcers that he is now a member of your pack. Usually a family room, the kitchen or a nearby adjoining breakfast area is ideal for providing safety and security for both puppy and owner.

Within that room, there should be a smaller area that your Dachshund can call his own. An alcove; a wire or fiberglass dog crate; or a fenced (not boarded!) corner from which he can view the activities of his new family will be fine. The size of the area or crate is the key factor here. The area must be large enough for your Dachsie to lie down and stretch out his super-long little body, yet small enough so that he cannot relieve himself at one end and sleep at the other without coming into contact with his droppings before he is fully trained to relieve himself outside.

Remember: Dogs are, by nature, clean animals and will not remain close to their relief areas unless forced to do so. In those cases, they then become dirty dogs and usually remain that way for life.

The designated area should be lined with clean bedding and a toy. Water must

Did You Know?

White vinegar is a good odor remover if you don't have any professional cleaners on hand; use one quarter cup to one quart of water.

always be available, in a nonspill container, once the dog is house-trained reliably.

SCHEDULE A SOLUTION

A puppy should be taken to his relief area each time he is released from his designated area, after meals, after play, and when he first awakens in the morning (at age eight weeks, this can mean 5 a.m.!). The puppy will indi-

This Dachsie crossbreed is smarter than most mutts, though not much taller!

cate that he's ready "to go" by circling or sniffing busily—do not misinterpret these signs. For a puppy younger than 10 weeks of age, a routine of taking him out every hour is necessary. As the puppy grows, he will be able to wait for longer periods of time.

Keep trips to his relief area short. Stay no more than five or six minutes and then return to the house. If he goes during that time, praise him lavishly and take him indoors immediately. If he does not, but he has an accident when you go back indoors, pick him up immediately, say "No! No!" and return to his relief area. Wait a few minutes, then return to the house again. Never hit a puppy or rub his face in urine or excrement when he has had an accident.

Once indoors, put your Dachsie in his crate until you clean up his accident. Then release him to the family area and watch him more closely than before. Chances are, his accident was a result of your not picking up his signals or waiting too long before offering him the opportunity to relieve himself. Never hold a grudge for accidents.

Let the puppy learn that going outdoors means it is time to relieve himself, not to play. Once trained, he will be able to play indoors and out and still differentiate between the times for play versus the times for relief.

Help your Dachshund develop regular hours for naps, being alone, playing by himself, and resting, all in his crate. Encourage him to entertain himself while you are busy with your activities. Let him learn that having

There are basically two options for potty training: indoor and outdoor (opposite page).

you nearby is comforting, but it is not your main purpose in life to provide him with undivided attention.

Each time you put your puppy in his own area, use the same cue, whatever suits you best. Soon he will run to his crate or special area when he hears you say those words.

Crate-training provides safety for you, your puppy and your home. It also provides your Dachsie with a feeling of security, and that helps him achieve self-confidence and clean habits.

Remember that one of the primary ingredients in house-training your puppy is control. Regardless of your lifestyle, there will always be occasions when you will need to have a place where your dog can stay and be happy and safe. Crate-training is the answer for now and in the future.

A few key elements are really all you need for a successful house-training method for your Dachshund: consistency, frequency, praise, control, and supervision. By following these procedures with a normal, healthy Dachsie puppy, you and he will soon be past the stage of "accidents" and ready to move on to a full and rewarding life together.

Having house-training problems with your Dachshund?
Ask other Dachsie owners for advice and tips. Log onto **DogChannel.com/Club-Dachsie** and click on "community."

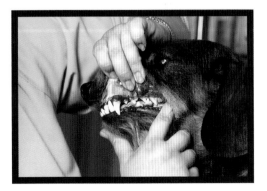

S electing a veterinarian should be based on personal recommendation, for the doctor's skills with dogs, and, if possible, familiarity with Dachshunds. It will be helpful if the vet is based nearby, because you might have an emergency or need to make multiple visits for treatments.

FIRST STEP: SELECT THE RIGHT VET

All licensed veterinarians are capable of dealing with routine medical issues such as infections, injuries, and the promotion of health (for example, by vaccinations). If the problem affecting your dog is more complex, your veterinarian may refer your pet to someone with a more detailed specialist like a veterinary dermatologist, veterinary ophthalmologist, etc. Specialists see certain problems hundreds of times, while vets may only encounter the problem a few times in his whole career.

It's not newsworthy that veterinary procedures are very costly and, new technologies and equipment are even more expensive. It is quite acceptable to discuss matters of cost with your vet; if there is more than one treatment option, cost may be a factor in deciding which route to take. Look into veterinary insurance as soon as your puppy arrives. Having a good insurance policy will remove the financial considerations from the equation if a major procedure or treatment becomes necessary.

To begin, look for a new veterinarian before you actually need one. For newbie pet owners, ideally start looking for a vet a month or two before you bring home your new Dachshund puppy. That will give you time to meet several veterinarians, check out the condition of the clinic and see who you

feel most comfortable with. If you already have a Dachsie, look sooner rather than later, preferably not in the midst of a health crisis.

Second, lists the traits that are important to you. Points to consider or investigate:

Convenience: Proximity to your home, extended hours or drop-off services are helpful for people who work regular business hours, have a busy schedule or don't want to drive far. If you have mobility issues, finding a veterinarian who makes house calls or a service that provides pet transport might be particularly important.

Size: A one-person practice ensures that you'll always be dealing with the same veterinarian during each and every visit. "That person can really get to know you and your dog," says Bernadine Cruz, D.V.M., of Laguna Hills Animal Hospital in California. The downside, though, is the sole practitioner does not have the immediate input of another veterinarian, and if your vet becomes ill or takes time off, you're out of luck.

The multiple-doctor practice offers consistency if your pet needs to come in unexpectedly on a day when your veterinarian isn't

---

there. Additionally, veterinarians can quickly consult with their colleagues within the clinic if they're unsure about a diagnosis or treatment.

If you find a veterinarian within that practice who you really like, you can make your appointments with that individual, establishing the same kind of bond that you would with the solo practitioner.

Appointment Policies: Some practices are strictly by-appointment only, which could minimize your wait time. However, if a sudden problem arises with your Dachsie and the vets are booked, they might not be able to squeeze your pet in that day. Some clinics are drop-in only—great for impromptu or crisis visits, but without scheduling , they may involve longer waits to see the next available veterinarian. Some practices maintain an appointment schedule but also keep slots open

Choosing a reputable vet and establishing a good relationship will benefit your dog for years to come.

throughout the day for walk-ins, offering the best of both worlds.

Basic vs. State-of-the-Art vs. Full-Service: A practice with high-tech equipment offers greater diagnostic capabilities and treatment options, important for tricky or difficult cases. However, the cost of pricey equipment gets passed along to the client, so you could pay a little more for routine procedures—the bulk of most pets' appointments. Some practices offer boarding, grooming, training classes and other services right on the premises, a convenience smart owners appreciate.

Fees and Payment Polices: How much is a routine office call? If there is a significant price difference? If so, ask why. If you intend to carry health insurance on your Dachsie or want to pay by credit card, make sure the clinic accepts those payment options beforehand.

FIRST VET VISIT

It is much easier, less costly and more effective to practice preventive medicine than to fight bouts of illness and disease. Properly bred puppies of all breeds come from parents who were selected for their good health as well as sound temperament and typical Dachsie appearance. The puppies' mother should have been vaccinated, free of all internal and external parasites, and properly nourished. Puppies gain disease-

A healthy dog begins with
a health-conscientious owner.

resistance from their mother, though it's possible that she's passed some internal parasites to her puppies. This is no cause for alarm as routine worming will remedy the puppies' systems.

Now that you have your Dachshund puppy home safe and sound, it's time to arrange your pup's first trip to the veterinarian. Perhaps the breeder can recommend someone who has a good reputation, or maybe you know other dog owners who can suggest a good vet. Either way, you should make an appointment within a couple of days of bringing home your Dachshund.

Your pup's first vet visit will consist of an overall examination to make sure that the pup does not have any problems that are not apparent to you. The veterinarian will also set up a schedule for your pup's vaccinations; the breeder will inform you of which ones the pup has already received, and the vet can continue from there.

NOTABLE & QUOTABLE

Weight control is really important to prevent back injuries. Dachsies have a propensity to become overweight, and that extra weight puts a lot of extra pressure on the spine. It's also wise not to teach your Dachshund behavior that will increase strain on his back—such as jumping from couches, beds, and steps.
—*Rick Parsons, D.V.M., of the Placerville Veterinary Clinic in Placerville, Calif.*

The puppy also will have his teeth examined and have his skeletal conformation and general health checked prior to certification by the veterinarian. Puppies in certain breeds have problems with their kneecaps, cataracts and other eye problems, heart murmurs, and undescended testicles. They may also have personality problems, something a veterinarian with training in temperament can evaluate.

VACCINATION SCHEDULING

Most vaccinations are given by injection and should only be administered by a veterinarian. Both you and the vet should keep a record of the date of the injection, the identification of the vaccine, and the amount given. Some vets give a first vaccination at eight weeks of age, but most dog breeders prefer the course not to commence until about ten weeks because of interaction with the antibodies produced by the mother. The vaccination scheduling is usually based on a fifteen-day cycle. You must take your vet's advice as to when to vaccinate, as this may differ according to the vaccine used.

The usual vaccines contain immunizing doses of several different viruses such as distemper, parvovirus, parainfluenza, and hepatitis. Other vaccines may been needed depending on regional viruses that may put your puppy at risk. Ask your vet.

This is especially true for the booster immunizations. Most vaccination programs require a booster when the puppy is a year old and once a year thereafter. In some cases, circumstances may require more frequent immunizations.

Puppies are immunized against canine cough, more formally known as tracheobronchitis, with a vaccine that is sprayed into the dog's nostrils. Canine cough is usually included in routine vaccinations, but it is often not as effective as the vaccines for other major diseases.

Your veterinarian will probably recommend that your puppy be fully vaccinated before you bring him outside. There are airborne diseases, parasite eggs in the grass, and unexpected visits from other dogs that might be dangerous to your puppy's health. Other dogs are the most harmful reservoir of pathogenic organisms, as everything they have can be transmitted to your puppy.

Five Months to One Year of Age: Unless you intend to breed or show your dog, neutering your puppy at six months of age is recommended. Discuss this with your veterinarian. Neutering/spaying has proven to be extremely beneficial to male and female puppies, respectively. Besides eliminating the possibility of pregnancy, it reduces the risk of breast cancer in females and prostate cancer in male dogs.

Your vet should provide your puppy with a thorough dental evaluation at six months of age, ascertaining whether all the permanent teeth have erupted properly. A home dental care regimen should be initiated at six months, including weekly brushing and providing toys and devices that promote good dental health (such as nylon bones). Regular dental care promotes healthy teeth, fresh breath, and a longer life.

Dogs Older Than One Year: Continue to visit the veterinarian at least once a year. There is no such disease as "old age," but bodily functions do change as your Dachsie ages. His eyes and ears are no longer as efficient. Liver, kidney, and intes-

Even if your dog is healthy, he should still receive regular checkups.

NOTABLE & QUOTABLE

These little breeds sometimes retain their baby teeth, and when that happens, the veterinarian has to put the dog under anesthesia to remove those teeth. Instead of putting them under twice—once for the early spay or neuter and then again to remove retained baby teeth—I recommend doing the spay or neuter after age six months when all the adult teeth are in. Then, while the puppy is anesthetized, the veterinarian can look for extra teeth and remove them at the same time.

—Bernadine Cruz, D.V.M., of Laguna Hills Animal Hospital in California

Puppies will have to visit the veterinarian more often than older dogs, who only visit the vet about once a year.

tinal functions often decline. Proper dietary changes, recommended by your veterinarian, can make life more pleasant for your aging Dachshund and you.

EVERYDAY ESSENTIALS

Keeping your Dachshund healthy is a matter of keen observation and quick action when necessary. Knowing what's normal for your dog will help you recognize signs of trouble before they blossom into a full-blown emergency situation.

Even if the problem is minor, such as a cut or scrape, you'll want to care for it immediately to prevent subsequent infec-

tions, as well as to ensure that your dog doesn't make it worse by chewing or scratching at it. Here's what to do for common, minor injuries or illnesses, and how to recognize and deal with emergencies.

Cuts and Scrapes: For a cut or scrape that's half an inch or smaller, clean the wound with saline solution or warm water and use tweezers to remove any splinters or other debris. Apply antibiotic ointment. No bandage is necessary unless the wound is on a paw, which can pick up dirt when your dog walks on it. Deep cuts that bleed a lot or those caused by glass or some other object should be treated by your veterinarian.

JOIN OUR ONLINE **Dachsie Club**

Just like with infants, puppies need a series of vaccinations to ensure that they stay healthy during their first year of life. Download a vaccination chart from **DogChannel.com/Club-Dachsie** that you can use to keep tract of your Dachsie's shots.

A healthy Dachsie has clear eyes, a shiny coat, and lots of energy.

Cold Symptoms: Dogs don't actually get colds, but they can get illnesses that have similar symptoms, such as coughing, a runny nose, or sneezing. Dogs cough for any number of reasons, from respiratory infections to inhaled irritants to congestive heart failure. Take your dog to the veterinarian for prolonged coughing, or coughing accompanied by labored breathing, runny eyes or nose, or bloody phlegm.

A runny nose that continues for more than several hours requires veterinary attention. If your Dachsie sneezes, he may have some mild nasal irritation that will resolve on its own, but frequent sneezing, especially if it's accompanied by a runny nose, may indicate anything from allergies to an infection to something stuck in the nose.

Vomiting and Diarrhea: Sometimes dogs suffer minor gastric upsets such as vomiting or diarrhea when they eat a new type of food, eat too much, get into the garbage, or become excited or anxious. Withhold food for twelve hours, then feed a bland diet such as baby food or rice and chicken, gradually returning the dog to his normal diet. Projectile vomiting, or vomiting or diarrhea that continues for more than 48 hours, is another matter. Your dog should be seen by the veterinarian.

Be on the lookout for back abnormalities, as Dachshunds are prone to spine problems.

It's important to feel comfortable with your vet of choice because he will be an integral part of your dog's life.

No matter how careful you are with your darling Dachsie, sometimes unexpected injuries happen. Be prepared for any emergency by creating a canine first-aid kit. Find out what essentials you need on **DogChannel.com/Club-Dachsie**—click on "downloads."

Whether your Dachsie wears a smooth, long, or wiry coat, or is of the standard or miniature variety, you can expect many years of great companionship from this playful little charmer. A healthy and vigorous breed, wiener dogs generally achieve a twelve- to eighteen-year lifespan.

SKIN PROBLEMS

Veterinarians are consulted by dog owners for skin problems more than for any other group of diseases or maladies. A dog's skin is as sensitive, if not more so, than human skin, and both suffer almost the same ailments (though the occurrence of acne in most breeds of dog is rare!). For this reason, veterinary dermatology has developed into a specialty.

Because many skin problems have visual symptoms that are almost identical, it requires the skill of an experienced veterinary dermatologist to identify and cure many of the more severe skin disorders. Pet-supply stores sell many treatments for skin problems, but most of the treatments are directed at symptoms and not at the underlying problem(s). If your dog is suffering from a skin disorder, seek professional assistance as quickly as possi-

it's a Fact

Dogs can get Lyme disease, Rocky Mountain spotted fever, tick bite paralysis, and many other diseases from ticks.

Dachshunds are at increased risk for intervertebral disk disease. Besides keeping your Dachsie at a proper weight, you can reduce spinal stress by properly lifting and carrying your dog (don't let his bottom dangle in the air; place one hand under his front legs and another hand under his bottom), and by keeping him from jumping on and off of furniture, in and out of cars, etc.

ble. As with all diseases, the earlier a problem is identified and treated, the more likely that the cure will be successful.

Many skin disorders are inherited, and smart Dachshund breeders are aware of these, as well as of those that derive from unknown causes. Sebaceous adenitis, a common skin problem in the Poodle, also affects the Dachshund, as does cutaneous asthenia, black-hair follicular dysplasia, body fold dermatitis, pinnal alopecia, and pattern alopecia. Not all of these are congenital diseases like sebaceous adenitis, but some hereditary links are suspected. Discuss these disorders with your breeder to find out if any of them have ever occurred in his line.

All inherited diseases must be diagnosed and treated by a veterinary specialist. There are active programs being undertaken by many veterinary pharmaceutical manufacturers to solve most, if not all, of the common skin problems in dogs.

PARASITE BITES

Many of us are allergic to insect bites. The bites itch, erupt, and may even become infected. Dogs have the same reaction to fleas, ticks, and/or mites. When an insect lands on you, you have the chance to whisk it away with your hand. Unfortunately, when a dog is bitten by a flea, tick, or mite, it can only scratch it away or bite it. By the time the dog has been bitten, the parasite has done some damage. It may also have laid eggs, which will cause further problems. The itching from parasite bites is probably due to the saliva injected into the site when the parasite sucks the dog's blood.

AIRBORNE ALLERGIES

Just as some humans suffer from hay fever during the pollinating season, many dogs suffer from the same allergies. When the pollen count is high, your dog might suffer but don't expect him to sneeze or have a runny nose like a human. Dogs react to pollen allergies in the same way they react to fleas; they scratch and bite themselves. Dogs, like humans, can be tested for allergens. Discuss the testing with your veterinarian.

AUTO-IMMUNE ILLNESS

An auto-immune illness is one in which the immune system overacts and does not recognize parts of the affected person; rather, the immune system starts to react as if these parts were foreign and need to be destroyed. An example is rheumatoid arthritis, which occurs when the body does not recognize the joints, thus leading to a very painful and damaging reaction in the joints. This has nothing to do with age, so it can occur in puppies. (The wear-and-tear arthritis of the older person or dog is called osteoarthritis.)

Lupus is another auto-immune disease that affects dogs and people. It can take variable forms, affecting the kidneys, bones, and the skin. It is treated with steroids, which can themselves have very significant side effects. Steroids calm the allergic reaction to the body's tissues, which helps the lupus, but also slow the body's reaction to real foreign substances such as bacteria. Steroids also thin the skin and bones.

FOOD ALLERGIES

Feeding your dog properly is very important. An incorrect diet could affect the dog's health, behavior, and nervous system, possibly making a normal dog into an aggressive one. Its most visible effects are to the skin and coat, but internal organs are similarly affected.

Dogs are allergic to many foods that are best-sellers and highly recommended by breeders and veterinarians. Changing the brand of food that you buy may not eliminate the problem if the element to which the dog is allergic is contained in the new brand.

Recognizing a food allergy can be difficult. Humans often have rashes when they eat foods to which they are allergic, or have swelling of the lips or eyes. Dogs do not usually develop rashes, but react in the same way as they to an airborne or bite allergy—they itch, scratch, and bite. While pollen allergies and parasite bites are usually seasonal, pollen allergies are year-round problems.

Some Dachsies are prone to diseases of the spine, which can be very painful.

Diagnosis of a food allergy is based on a two- to four-week dietary trial with a home-cooked diet fed to the exclusion of all other foods. The diet should consist of boiled rice or potato with a source of protein that the dog has never eaten before, such as fresh or frozen fish, lamb, or even something as exotic as pheasant. Water must be the only liquid available, and it is important that no other foods are fed during this trial. If the dog's condition improves, you will need to try the original diet once again to see if the itching resumes. If it does, then this confirms the diagnosis that the dog is allergic to its original diet. The treatment is long-term feeding of something that does not distress the dog's skin, which may be in the form of one of the commercially available hypoaller-genic diets or the homemade diet that you created for the allergy trial.

Food intolerance is the inability of the dog to completely digest certain foods. This occurs because the dog does not have the chemicals (enzymes) necessary to digest some foodstuffs. All puppies have the enzymes necessary to digest canine milk, but some dogs do not have the enzymes to digest a very different form of milk that is

Like humans, some Dachsies are allergic to pollen and other outside irritants.

commonly found in human households—milk from cows. In such dogs, drinking cows' milk results in loose bowels, stomach pains, and the passage of gas.

Dogs often do not have the enzymes to digest soy or other beans. The treatment is to exclude the foodstuffs that upset your Dachshund's stomach.

EXTERNAL PARASITES

Fleas: Of all the problems to which dogs are prone, none is better known and frustrating than fleas. Flea infestation is relatively simple to cure but difficult to prevent. Parasites that are harbored inside the body are a bit more difficult to eradicate but they are easier to control.

To control flea infestation, you have to understand the flea's life cycle. Fleas are often thought of as a summertime problem, but centrally heated homes have changed that, and fleas can be found at any time of the year. The most effective method of flea control is a two-stage approach: one stage to kill the adult fleas, and the other to control the development of pre-adult fleas. Unfortunately, no single active ingredient is effective against all stages of the life cycle.

Treating fleas should be a two-pronged attack. First, the environment needs to be treated; this includes carpets and furniture, especially the dog's bedding and areas underneath furniture. The environment should be treated

Fleas and ticks affect a lot of dogs, so the best bet is to prevent them before they take up residence on your Dachsie.

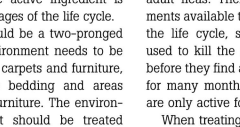

Did You Know?

Across the globe, more than 800 species of ticks exist, and they aren't particular to where they dine. Mammals, birds, and reptiles are all fair game.

with a household spray containing an Insect Growth Regulator and an insecticide to kill the adult fleas. Most IGRs are effective against eggs and larvae; they actually mimic the fleas' own hormones and stop the eggs and larvae from developing into adult fleas. There are currently no treatments available to attack the pupae stage of the life cycle, so the adult insecticide is used to kill the newly hatched adult fleas before they find a host. Most IGRs are active for many months, while adult insecticides are only active for a few days.

When treating with a household spray, it is a good idea to vacuum before applying the product. This stimulates as many pupae as possible to hatch into adult fleas. The vacuum cleaner should also be treated with an insecticide to prevent the eggs and larvae that have been collected in the vacuum bag from hatching.

The second stage of treatment is to apply an adult insecticide to the dog. Tra-

Though fleas and ticks can be treated topically, internal parasites require medications.

ditionally, this would be in the form of a collar or a spray, but more recent innovations include digestible insecticides that poison the fleas when they ingest the dog's blood. Alternatively, there are drops that, when placed on the back of the dog's neck, spread throughout the hair and skin to kill adult fleas.

Ticks: Though not as common as fleas, ticks are found all over the tropical and temperate world. They don't bite, like fleas; they harpoon. They dig their sharp proboscis (nose) into the dog's skin and drink the blood. Their only food and drink is dog's blood. They are controlled the same way fleas are controlled.

The American dog tick, *Dermacentor variabilis*, may well be the most common dog tick in many geographical areas, especially those areas where the climate is hot and humid. Most dog ticks have life expectancies

of a week to six months, depending upon climatic conditions. Ticks cannot jump or fly, but they can crawl slowly and can range up to 16 feet to reach a sleeping or unsuspecting dog.

Mites: Mites can also be an itchy nuisance. Microscopic in size, mites are related to ticks and generally take up permanent residence on their host animal—in this case, your Dachsie! The term "mange" refers to any infestation caused by one of the mighty mites, of which there are six varieties that concern smart dog owners.

■ *Demodex* mites cause a condition known as demodicosis (sometimes called red mange or follicular mange), in which the mites live in the dog's hair follicles and sebaceous glands in larger-than-normal numbers. Most dogs recover from this type of mange without any treatment, though topical therapies are commonly prescribed by the vet.

■ The *Cheyletiellosis* mite is the hook-mouthed culprit associated with "walking dandruff," a condition that affects dogs as well as cats and rabbits. If not treated, this mange can affect a whole kennel of dogs and can be spread to humans as well.

■ The *Sarcoptes* mite causes intense itching on the dog in the form of a condition known as scabies or sarcoptic mange. Scabies is highly contagious and can be passed to humans. Sometimes an allergic reaction to the mite worsens the severe itching associated with sarcoptic mange.

■ Ear mites, *Otodectes cynotis*, lead to otodectic mange, which commonly affects the outer ear canal of the dog, though other areas can be affected as well. Your vet can prescribe a treatment to flush out the ears and kill any eggs in the ears. A complete month of treatment is necessary to cure the mange.

■ Two other mites, less common in dogs, include *Dermanyssus gallinae* (the poultry or red mite) and *Eutrombicula alfreddugesi* (the North American mite associated with trombiculidiasis or chigger infestation). The types of mange caused by both of these mites are treatable by vets.

INTERNAL PARASITES

Most animals—fish, birds, and mammals, including dogs and humans—have worms and other parasites that live inside their bodies. According to Dr. Herbert R. Axelrod, a fish pathologist, there are two kinds of parasites: dumb and smart. The smart parasites live in peaceful cooperation with their hosts (symbiosis), while the dumb parasites kill their hosts. Most worm infections are relatively easy to control. If they are not controlled, they weaken the host dog to the point that other medical problems occur, but they do not kill the host as dumb parasites would.

Roundworms: The roundworms that infect dogs live in the dog's intestines and shed eggs continually. A dog produces about six or more ounces of feces every day. Each ounce of feces averages hundreds of thousands of roundworm eggs. All areas in which dogs roam contain roundworm eggs. The greatest danger of roundworms is that they infect people, too! It is smart to have your dog tested regularly for roundworms.

Roundworm infection can kill puppies and cause severe problems in adults, as the hatched larvae travel to the lungs and trachea through the bloodstream. Cleanliness is the best preventative for roundworms.

Most worm infections are easy to control with medication.

Always pick up after your dog and dispose of feces in appropriate receptacles.

Hookworms: Hookworms are dangerous to humans as well as to dogs and cats, and can be the cause of severe anemia due to iron deficiency. The worm uses its teeth to attach itself to the dog's intestines and changes the site of its attachment about six times per day. Each time the worm repositions itself, the dog loses blood and can become anemic.

Symptoms of hookworm infection include dark stools, weight loss, general weakness, pale coloration and anemia, as well as possible skin problems. Fortunately, hookworms are easily purged from the affected dog with a number of medications that have proven effective. Discuss these with your vet. Most heartworm preventatives include a hookworm insecticide as well.

Smart owners must be aware that hookworms can infect humans, who can acquire the larvae through exposure to contaminated feces. Because the worms cannot complete their life cycle on a human, the worms simply infest the skin and cause irritation. As a preventative, use disposable gloves or a "poop-scoop" to pick up your dog's droppings and prevent your dog (or

neighborhood cats) from defecating in children's play areas.

Tapeworms: There are many species of tapeworm, all of which are carried by fleas. Fleas are so small that your dog could pass them onto your hands, your plate or your food and thus make it possible for you to ingest a flea that is carrying tapeworm eggs. While tapeworm infection is not life-threatening in dogs (smart parasite!), it can be the cause of a very serious liver disease for humans.

Whipworms: In North America, whipworms are counted among the most common parasitic worm in dogs. Affected dogs may only experience upset tummies, colic, and diarrhea. These worms, however, can live for months or years in the dog, beginning their larval stage in the small intestine, spending their adult stage in the large intestine and finally passing infective eggs through the dog's feces. The only way to detect whipworms is through a fecal examination,

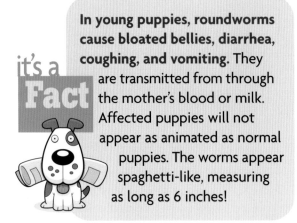

it's a Fact

In young puppies, roundworms cause bloated bellies, diarrhea, coughing, and vomiting. They are transmitted from through the mother's blood or milk. Affected puppies will not appear as animated as normal puppies. The worms appear spaghetti-like, measuring as long as 6 inches!

though this is not always foolproof. Treatment for whipworms is tricky, due to the worms' unusual life-cycle pattern, and very often dogs are reinfected due to exposure to infected eggs on the ground. Cleaning up droppings in your backyard as well as in public places is absolutely essential for sanitation purposes and the health of your dog and others.

Heartworms: Heartworms are thin, extended worms up to 12 inches long, which live in a dog's heart and the major blood vessels surrounding it. Dogs may have up to 200 worms. Symptoms may be loss of energy, loss of appetite, coughing, the development of a pot belly, and anemia.

Heartworms are transmitted by mosquitoes. The mosquito drinks the blood of an infected dog and takes in larvae with the blood. The larvae, called *microfilariae*, develop within the body of the mosquito and are passed on to the next dog bitten after the larvae mature. It takes two to three weeks for the larvae to develop to the infectious stage within the body of the mosquito. Dogs are usually treated at about six weeks of age and maintained on a prophylactic dose given monthly.

Blood testing for heartworms is not necessarily indicative of how seriously your dog is infected. Although this is a dangerous disease, it is not easy for a dog to be infected. Discuss the various preventatives with your vet because many types are available. Together you can decide on a safe course of prevention for your dog. Depending on where you live, you may need to keep your Dachshund on preventatives all year long.

DACHSHUND HEALTH DILEMMAS

Like all purebred and mixed breeds, Dachshunds carry genetic defects—genes

that can cause hereditary disease—which make them susceptible to certain genetic disorders. Hereditary diseases that may trouble the Dachshund include canine intervertebral disk disease, progressive retinal atrophy, and epilepsy. Although the odds are good that your Dachsie will never encounter these problems, particularly if he came from a health-conscious breeder who follows good breeding practices, you should be familiar with these disorders in order to recognize early signs and to initiate timely and appropriate veterinary treatment.

Intervertebral disk disease affects more Dachshunds than all other dogs combined, so naturally it is at the top of this list of conditions that concern smart Dachshund owners. Due to the Dachshund's long-backed construction, owners are advised to avoid activities that will strain their dog's back and spine. IVDD, as the disease is known, is marked by herniated disks in the lower back. The disease primarily affects dogs with stunted legs. Affected dogs experience severe pain, usually in the lower back but sometimes in the neck as well. The disease can be treated medically and/or surgically, depending on the severity. Carts for dogs have been devised to assist Dachshunds with rear-quarter paralysis due to severe IVDD.

Acanthosis nigricans, a skin disorder unique to the Dachshund, is characterized by dark, thick skin in Dachshund's groin and armpits. While the genetic origin of the disease is unclear, it is certain that affected dogs are not to be bred. Vitamin E supplementation has been used to improve the condition, though no cure is known.

Hypothyroidism, commonly confused with obesity in Dachshunds, is simply the insufficient production of thyroid hormones. In Dachshunds, lymphocytic thyroiditis is

Dachsie owners must not overexert their dogs or make them do anything that may harm their back.

most common. Dogs are affected between the ages of one to three. Less than half of the Dachshunds affected manifest obesity; most experience recurrent infections and lack of energy. Diagnosis of hypothyroidism is often tricky, though the treatment tends to be direct and affordable.

Epilepsy is a seizure disorder that affects Dachshunds as well as many other breeds. Epileptic dogs can be managed with various drugs, though some side effects exist, including temporary weakness and increased appetite and thirst.

EYE PROBLEMS

Any breed of dog can be prone to eye problems, and the Dachshund is no exception. Some basic knowledge of common eye problems can prove useful for all smart Dachsie owners. Perhaps the most frequently encountered eye problem seen in Dachshunds, especially older dogs, is cataracts. A cataract is a cloudiness or film over the lens of the eye, categorized by age of onset, location on the eye, and stage of the cloudiness. As it is a hereditary condition, parents should be tested before breeding to ensure that they are not carrying the genes for cataracts.

Glaucoma, a leading cause of blindness in dogs, is caused by an increase in fluid pressure within the eye. This disease can be hereditary, so parents should be tested prior to breeding. Treatment for glaucoma can be medical or surgical, or both.

Progressive retinal atrophy, a series of inherited disorders affecting the retina of the eyes, causes visual impairment that is slow but progressive. Night blindness can be the first sign of trouble. There is no known way to stop onset.

Other eye conditions have also been known to occur in Dachshunds. This list is by

One good way to ensure your puppy is free from genetic problems is to get your Dachsie from a good breeder.

no means complete, but is included here to make new owners aware of possible problems in the breed: corneal dystrophy, congenital night blindness, entropion, tear duct anomalies, walleye, keratoconjunctivitis, microphthalmia, and ectasia syndrome.

Discuss the following conditions with your veterinarian and/or breeder. A better understanding of each of these problems will enlighten the new owner, making him more aware of the breed's congenital, hereditary and environmentally triggered problems. These potential problems include excessive hardening of the long bones, osteoporosis, cutaneous asthenia (also known as Ehlers-Danlos syndrome), renal hypoplasia (problem of the kidneys), diabetes, urinary tract problems, and achondroplasia (a genetic bone disease). Hair changes, sluggishness, and secondary infections are common signs of potential problems and must be treated aggressively by a veterinarian. Smart owners should be aware that deafness in dappled dogs and von Willebrand's disease (a common blood disease) are genetic.

M ost Dachshund people will attest that the breed is not populated with finicky eaters. Dachsies love to eat so finding a food that your dog will enjoy is hardly a challenge. Fortunately for smart owners and ever-hungry Dachsies, the choices of dog food are nearly endless. A visit to the local pet-supply store will reveal dozens of brands of food in all sorts of flavors and textures, ranging from puppy diets to those for seniors. There are even hypoallergenic and low-calorie diets available.

Because your Dachshund's food has a bearing on his coat, health, and temperament, it is essential that the most suitable diet is selected for a Dachshund of his age. It is fair to say, however, that even experienced owners can be perplexed by the enormous range of foods available. Understanding what is best for your dog will help you reach an informed decision.

BASIC TYPES

Dog foods are produced in various types: dry, wet (canned), semimoist, fresh packaged, and frozen. Dry foods are useful for the

it's a Fact Bones can cause gastrointestinal obstruction and perforation, and may be contaminated with salmonella or E. coli. Leave them in the trash and give your dog a nylon bone toy instead.

cost-conscious, because they tend to be less expensive than the others. They also contain the least fat and the most preservatives. Dry food also takes longer to eat than other foods, so it's more filling.

Wet food—available in cans or foil pouches—is more expensive and generally are made up of sixty to seventy percent water. A palatable source of concentrated nutrition, wet food makes a good supplement for underweight dogs or those recovering from illness. Some dog owners even add a little wet food to dry food to increase its appeal.

Semimoist food is flavorful but usually contains lots of sugar, which can lead to dental problems and obesity. It's not a good choice for your sausage dog's main diet.

You can also find small logs of fresh food, some of which require refrigeration, at pet-supply stores. Many Dachshunds find this food more palatable than any other, though it is expensive. Likewise, frozen food, which

is available in cooked and raw forms, is usually more expensive than wet foods. The advantages of frozen food are similar to those of wet foods.

Some manufacturers have developed special foods for small dogs. Some of these contain slightly more protein, fat, and calories than standard foods. Manufacturers contend that small dogs need these additional nutrients to fuel their active lifestyle and revved-up metabolism. In reality, your hound may or may not need them; the

The amount of food your Dachsie eats should depend on how active he is. A lazy dog does not need as much food as an active one.

nutritional needs of dogs vary considerably, even within the same breed. It's OK to feed your Dachsie small-breed food, but standard food will provide balanced nutrition, too, as long as you feed appropriate amounts tailored to your buddy's needs.

Some dry foods for small dogs have compositions that are identical to those for larger dogs, but the kibble size is smaller to make it easier to chew. Small dogs don't really need smaller kibble, though your dog may prefer it. Many small dogs eat standard-size kibble with no trouble at all.

The amount of food your Dachshund needs depends on a number of factors, such as age, activity level, food quality, reproductive status, and size. What is the easiest way to figure it out? Start with the manufacturer's recommended amount, then adjust it according to your Dachsie's response. For example, if you feed the recommended amount for a few weeks and your Dachshund loses weight, increase the amount by ten to twenty percent. If your dog gains weight, decrease the amount. It won't take long to determine the amount of food that keeps your little friend in optimal condition.

NUTRITION 101

All Dachshunds (and all dogs, for that matter) need proteins, carbohydrates, fats, vitamins, and minerals for optimal growth and health.

■ **Proteins** are used for growth and repair of muscles, bones, and other bodily tissues. They're also used for production of antibodies, enzymes, and hormones. All dogs need protein, but it's especially important for puppies because they grow and develop so rapidly. Protein sources include various types of meat, meat meal, meat byproducts, eggs, dairy products, and soybeans.

■ **Carbohydrates** are metabolized into glucose, the body's main energy source. Carbohydrates are available as sugars, starches, and fiber.

◆ sugars (simple carbohydrates) are not suitable nutrient sources for dogs.

◆ starches—a preferred type of carbohy-drates in dog food—are found in a variety of plant products. Starches must be cooked in order to be digested.

◆ fiber (cellulose)—also a preferred type of carbohydrates in dog food—isn't digestible but helps the digestive tract function properly.

■ **Fats** are also used for energy and play an important role in skin and coat health, hormone production, nervous system function, and vitamin transport. Fat increases the palatability and the calorie count of food, which can lead to serious health problems, such as obesity, for dogs that are allowed to overindulge. Some foods contain added amounts of omega fatty acids such as do-cosohexaenoic acid, a compound that may enhance brain development and learning in puppies but is not considered an essential nutrient by the Association of American

Dogs need the proper amounts of nutrients in their food, including protein, carbs, fats, vitamins, and minerals.

All dogs love treats and people food, but these goodies can unbalance your Dachsie's diet and lead to a weight problem if you don't choose and feed them wisely. People food, whether fed as a treat or as part of a meal, shouldn't account for more than ten percent of your youngster's daily caloric intake. If you plan to give your Dachshund treats, be sure to include "treat calories" when calculating the daily food requirement—so you don't end up with a pudgy pup!

When shopping for packaged treats, look for ones that provide complete nutrition—they're basically dog food in a fun form. Choose crunchy goodies for chewing fun and dental health. Other ideas for tasty treats include:

✓ small chunks of cooked, lean meat
✓ dry dog food morsels
✓ cheese
✓ veggies (cooked or raw)
✓ bread, crackers or cereal
✓ plain, popped popcorn

Some foods, however, can be dangerous and even deadly to a dog. The following items can cause digestive upset (vomiting and/or diarrhea) or toxic reactions that could be fatal:

✗ **avocados:** can cause gastrointestinal irritation, with vomiting and diarrhea, if eaten in sufficient quantity

✗ **baby food:** may contain onion powder; does not provide balanced nutrition

✗ **chocolate:** contains methylxanthines and theobromine, caffeine-like compounds that can cause vomiting, diarrhea, heart abnormalities, tremors, seizures, and death. Darker chocolates contain higher levels of these toxic compounds.

✗ **eggs, raw:** whites contain an enzyme that prevents uptake of biotin, a B vitamin; may contain salmonella

✗ **garlic (and related foods):** can cause gastrointestinal irritation and anemia if eaten in sufficient quantity

✗ **grapes:** can cause kidney failure if eaten in sufficient quantity (the toxic dose varies from dog to dog)

✗ **macadamia nuts:** can cause vomiting, weakness, lack of coordination, and other symptoms

✗ **meat, raw:** may contain harmful bacteria such as salmonella or E. coli

✗ **milk:** can cause diarrhea in some puppies

✗ **onions (and related foods):** can cause gastrointestinal irritation and anemia if eaten in sufficient quantity

✗ **raisins:** can cause kidney failure if eaten in sufficient quantity (toxic dose varies from dog to dog)

✗ **yeast bread dough:** can rise in gastrointestinal tract, causing obstruction; produces alcohol as it rises

Along with good food, your dog should have access to plenty of clean water.

Feed Control Officials (www.aafco.org). Fats used in dog foods include tallow, lard, poultry fat, fish oil and vegetable oils.

■ **Vitamins** and **minerals** aid in muscle and nerve function, bone growth, healing, metabolism, and fluid balance. Especially important for your dog are calcium, phosphorus, and vitamin D, which must be supplied in the right balance to ensure proper development of bones and teeth.

Just as your Dachsie needs proper nutrition from his food, water is an essential "nutrient" as well. Water keeps your dog's body properly hydrated and promotes normal function of the body's systems. During house-training, it is necessary to keep an eye on how much water your Dachshund is drinking, but once he is reliably trained he should have access to clean, fresh water at all times, especially if you feed dry food. Make sure that your dog's water bowl is clean, and change the water often.

CHECK OUT THE LABEL

To help you understand what you are feeding your dog, start by taking a look at the label on the package or can. Look for the words "complete and balanced." This tells you that the food meets specific nutritional requirements set by the AAFCO for

JOIN OUR ONLINE Dachsie Club

Feeding your dog is part of your daily routine. Take a break and have some fun online and play "Feed the Dachsie," an exclusive game found only on **DogChannel.com/Club-Dachsie**—just click on "fun and games."

How can you tell if your Dachshund is fit or fat? When you run your hands down his sides from front to back, you should be able to easily feel his ribs. It's OK if you feel a little body fat (and, of course, a lot of hair), but you should not feel huge fat pads. You should also be able to feel your Dachsie's waist—an indentation behind the ribs.

either adults ("maintenance") or puppies and pregnant/lactating bitches ("growth and reproduction"). The label must state the group for which it is intended.

The label also includes a nutritional analysis, which lists minimum protein, minimum fat, maximum fiber, and maximum moisture content, as well as other information. (You won't find carbohydrate content, because it's everything that isn't protein, fat, fiber, and moisture.)

The nutritional analysis refers to crude protein and crude fat—amounts that have been determined in the laboratory. This analysis is technically accurate, but it doesn't tell you anything about digestibility: how much of the particular nutrient your Dachshund can actually use. For information about digestibility, contact the manufacturer (check the label for a telephone number and website address).

Virtually all commercial puppy foods exceed AAFCO's minimal requirements for protein and fat, the two nutrients most commonly evaluated when comparing foods. Protein levels in dry puppy foods usually range from about twenty-six to thirty percent; for canned foods, the values are about nine to thirteen percent. The fat content of dry puppy foods is about twenty percent or more; for canned foods, it's eight percent or more. (Dry food values are larger than canned food values because dry food contains less water; the values are actually similar when compared on a dry matter basis.)

Finally, check out the label's ingredient list, which lists the ingredients in descending order by weight. Manufacturers are allowed to list separately different forms of a single ingredient (e.g., ground corn and corn gluten meal). The food may contain things like meat byproducts, meat and bone meal, and animal fat, which probably won't appeal to you but are nutritious and safe for your Dachsie. Higher-quality foods usually have meat or meat products near the top of the ingredient list, but you don't need to worry about grain products as long as the label indicates that the food is nutritionally complete. Dogs are omnivores (not carnivores, as commonly believed), so all balanced dog foods contain animal and plant ingredients.

STAGES OF LIFE

When selecting your dog's diet, three stages of development must be considered: the puppy stage, the adult stage, and the senior stage.

PUPPY DIETS: Puppies instinctively want milk from their mother and a normal puppy will exhibit this behavior from just a few moments following birth. Puppies should be allowed to nurse from their mothers for about the first six weeks, although from the third or fourth week, the breeder will begin to introduce small portions of suitable solid food. Most breeders like to introduce alternate milk and meat meals initially, building up to weaning time.

By the time the puppies are seven or a maximum of eight weeks old, they should be fully weaned and fed solely on a proprietary puppy food. Selection of the most suitable, quality diet at this time is essential, because a puppy's fastest growth rate is during the first year of life. Ask your veterinarians for advice. The frequency of meals will be reduced over time, and when a young dog has reached the age of about ten to twelve months, he should be switched to an adult diet.

Puppy and junior diets can be well balanced for the needs of your Dachshund so that, except in certain circumstances, additional vitamins, minerals, and proteins will not be required.

ADULT DIETS: A dog is considered an adult when he has stopped growing, so in general, a Dachshund can be fed an adult diet at about ten to twelve months of age. Again, you should rely upon your veterinarian or dietary specialist to recommend an

A Dachsie can be switched to an adult diet after about ten to twelve months of age.

acceptable maintenance diet. Major dog food manufacturers specialize in this type of food, and it is merely necessary for you to select the one best suited to your dog's needs.

Because Dachshunds are more prone to obesity than many other breeds, smart owners must monitor their Dachsies' diets with special care. Neutered Dachshunds are twice as likely to become obese as unaltered dogs and should be fed a reduced-calorie food, designed for the obesity-prone. Owners should not leave the Dachshund's food out all day for "free-choice" feeding, as this freedom inevitably translates to inches around the dog's waist.

SENIOR DIETS: As dogs get older, their metabolism changes. An older dog usually exercises less, moves more slowly and sleeps more. This change in lifestyle and physiological performance requires a change in diet. Because these changes take place slowly, they might not be recognizable. These metabolic changes increase the tendency toward obesity, requiring an even more vigilant approach to feeding. Obesity in an older dog compounds the health problems that already accompany old age.

As your dog gets older, his kidneys slow down and his intestines become less efficient. These age-related factors are best handled with a change in diet and a change in feeding schedule to give smaller portions that are more easily digested.

There is no single best diet for every older dog. While many dogs do well on light or senior diets, other dogs do better on puppy diets or other special premium diets such as lamb and rice. Be sensitive to your senior Dachshund's diet, and this will help control other problems that may arise with your old friend.

As dogs get older, their food needs change.

These delicious, dog-friendly recipes will have your furry friend smacking his lips and salivating for more. Just remember: Treats aren't meant to replace your Dachsie's regular meals. Give your dog snacks sparingly and continue to feed him nutritious, well-balanced meals.

Cheddar Squares

$\frac{1}{3}$ cup all-natural applesauce
$\frac{1}{3}$ cup low-fat cheddar cheese, shredded
$\frac{1}{3}$ cup water
2 cups unbleached white flour

In a medium bowl, mix all wet ingredients. In a large bowl, mix all dry ingredients. Slowly add the wet ingredients to the dry mixture. Mix well. Pour batter into a greased 13x9x2-inch pan. Bake at 375-degrees Fahrenheit for 25 to 30 minutes. Bars are done when a toothpick inserted in the center and removed comes out clean. Cool and cut into bars. Makes about 54 one-and-a-half-inch bars.

Peanut Butter Bites

3 tablespoons vegetable oil
$\frac{1}{4}$ cup smooth peanut butter, no salt or sugar
$\frac{1}{4}$ cup honey
1 $\frac{1}{2}$ teaspoon baking powder
2 eggs
2 cups whole wheat flower

In a large bowl, mix all ingredients until dough is firm. If the dough is too sticky, mix in a small amount of flour. Knead dough on a lightly floured surface until firm. Roll out dough half an inch thick and cut with cookie cutters. Put cookies on a cookie sheet half an inch apart. Bake at 350-degrees Fahrenheit for 20 to 25 minutes. When done, cookies should be firm to the touch. Turn oven off and leave cookies for one to two hours to harden. Makes about 40 2-inch-long cookies.

Each Dachshund coat type—smooth, longhaired, and wirehaired—has its own grooming requirements, the smooth being the easiest to maintain. All grooming tools mentioned are available at pet-supply stores.

Smooth: Daily brushing with a rubber curry brush (an oval, plastic, handheld brush with small rubber nubs) or grooming mitt (a mitten with rubber nubs on the palm side) works well. Most Dachsies love the sensation of being rubbed; it stimulates their circulation and distributes healthy oils throughout their coat. In a hectic household, a once-a-week rubdown to remove loose hairs will suffice for these easiest of easy-to-groom dogs. A spray or rub with a coat gloss or chamois cloth will heighten that beautiful sheen.

Longhaired: For longhaired Dachshunds, a daily grooming session is ideal, with a thorough brushing at least twice a week. A favorite brush is the slicker, which has curved metal teeth. A doubled-sided steel comb is also recommended to locate any tangles your brush may miss. The mat-breaker, a small tool with removable, razor-sharp blades, is invaluable for splitting any mats that have

Did You Know? **Nail clipping can be tricky, so many owners leave the task for the professionals.** However, if you walk your dog on concrete, you may not have to worry about it. The concrete acts like a nail file and probably will keep the nails in check.

formed in your Dachshund's coat. Using a gentle, rocking stroke, you can work your way through these tangles, then brush them from the coat.

Use these tools carefully. With too heavy a hand, the slicker brush can burn and irritate tender skin. Grab a small portion of the dog's fur with one hand, insert the brush bristles into the hair next the skin, then gently pull the brush through that path of fur. Never yank at snarls and tangles. This hurts your dog as much as it would hurt you. Never use the mat-splitting tool in areas where it could cut skin, such as ear flaps, leg tendons, armpit folds, or the anal or genital areas. It's best to have a professional groomer demonstrate the proper use of this tool.

Begin brushing or combing at the same point on your dog's body each time you groom. Start on the dog's hindquarters, then work your way forward and down.

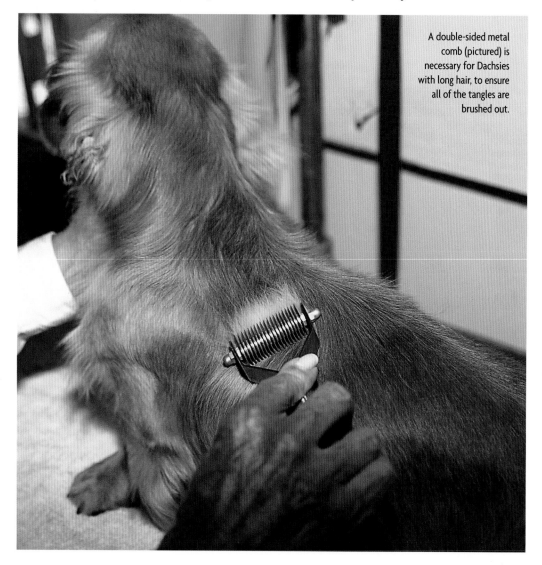

A double-sided metal comb (pictured) is necessary for Dachsies with long hair, to ensure all of the tangles are brushed out.

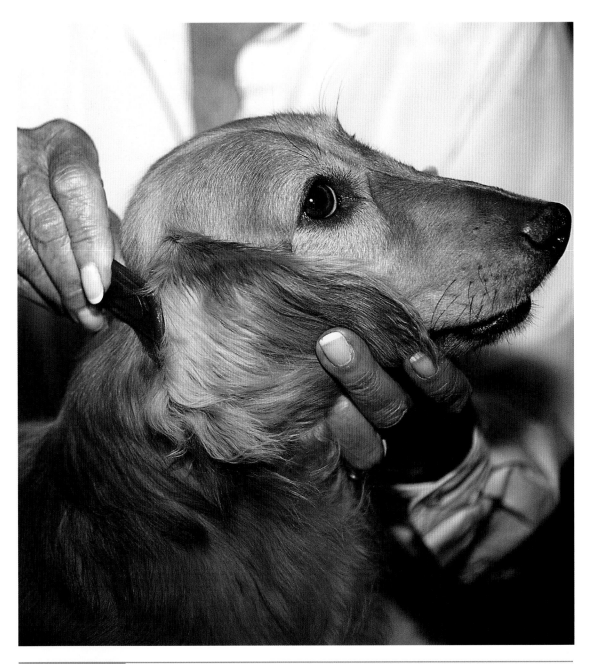

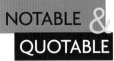
After removing a tick, clean the dog's skin with hydrogen peroxide. If Lyme disease is common where you live, have your veterinarian test the tick. Tick preventive medication will discourage ticks from attaching and kill any that do. —groomer Andrea Vilardi from West Paterson, N.J.

The wirehaired Dachshund is born smooth. As he matures, his coat becomes more profuse. The full, mature coat completely comes in at one to two years of age.

Because your own back requires as much consideration as your Dachshund's, a grooming table is a worthwhile investment. As you work your way around to the dog's front legs, you may want to lift them to reach the chest and armpit areas, but be careful not to twist or overextend them because this can damage ligaments.

Unless you've been taught how to groom a longhaired Dachshund, take your dog to a professional groomer every eight weeks. Properly grooming a longhaired Dachsie involves a combination of grooming techniques.

Handstripping, or carding, the coat with a stripping tool removes stray hairs and dead undercoat, which speeds up the shedding process. Plus, you'll need to expertly use thinning shears to tidy up the dog's profile. To perform these two techniques correctly, you need to understand the breed standard (a description of how the ideal dog should look) and possess the skill to use the required tools.

Bathe your Dachsie indoors in a sink or tub for maximum comfort for you both.

Dachsies are medium shedders, they are relatively clean, and they have minimal doggie odor. These low-riders often pick up mud and debris during their excursions, though. They love to roll in smelly substances when they come across them in their travels, a throwback to their hunting days when they masked their scent to prevent alerting their prey.—Kathy Salzberg, national certified master groomer and owner of The Village Groomer in Walpole, Mass.

Dachsies only need baths every once in awhile, such as when they romp in a puddle or start to smell.

Your dedication and time are still needed, however, to maintain your little longhaired beauty between visits to the groomer, so regular brushing is highly recommended. If you have the time and energy, schedule some sessions with a professional groomer or handler of this breed and take some trips to dog shows to observe the finished product in the ring. Groomers sometimes trim some length from the longhaired Dachshund's legs and furnishings (the longer hair on the dog's legs, ears and tail). This pet trim retains most of the dog's gorgeous locks and is much easier to maintain between visits.

Wirehaired: Viewed from a distance, the well-groomed wirehaired Dachshund resembles his smooth cousin, but this tailored profile doesn't just happen naturally. To preserve his harsh texture, handstripping is required and is usually performed by a groomer or, in the case of a show dog, by his handler. Performed with a stripping knife, thumb and fingers, handstripping is the systematic removal of dead coat. The result is a hard-as-nails coat that looks as if it naturally grew that way.

When this type of coat is not hand-stripped, the wirehaired Dachshund may end up looking more like a shaggy, short-legged version of Benji than his show-dog counterparts. If you have your wirehaired stripped every two or three months by a professional, you can help maintain him between visits by lightly stripping the coat on a weekly basis with a stripping knife, removing dead coat and allowing for constant new hair growth. You need to know what you're doing before you pick up that tool, though, so ask the groomer for a demonstration before you tackle this task.

For pet trims on wirehaired Dachshunds, some groomers achieve the same look as the show dogs by using their clippers. However, this grooming method doesn't maintain the coat's harsh texture, and a softer coat usually grows in. Whether the

SMART TIP!

Treats are useful in encouraging correct behavior, such as standing for grooming or nail trimming. With a Dachshund, the power of food is endless.

dog is stripped or clipped, the groomer will thin and shape the dog's beard and eyebrows to bring out the breed's trademark distinguished but rakish appearance.

To finish, the groomer trims the hair under the feet so it's even with the pads on wirehaireds and longhaireds. Straight scissors are used to trim hair around the foot, but

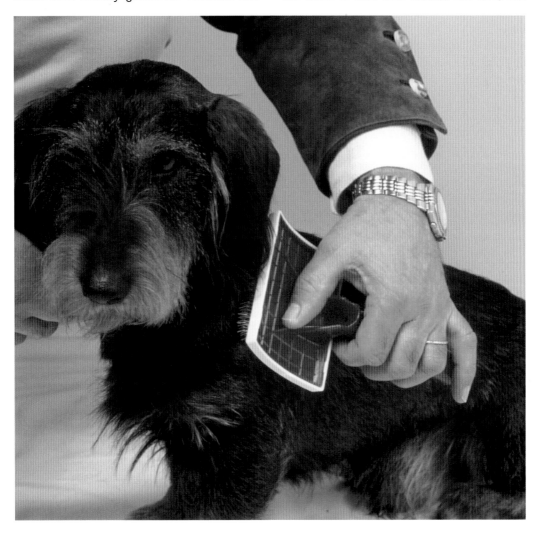

exposed nails or toes are undesirable. The foot should look neat, round, and compact.

Your job at home is to brush your wire-haired with a soft, straight-bristled slicker brush at least once a week to keep him tangle-free and to distribute the oils through his coat. One advantage of the wire coat is that it seldom gets dirty. A quick brushing is usually all it takes to remove dried mud or other "souvenirs" from his out-door exploits.

BATHING

Dachshunds don't need to be bathed often, provided that they are brushed on a regular schedule. Schedule baths several times a year and whenever your dog gets into something that creates an unpleasant odor. He can be washed, using a dog sham-poo. (Human shampoo dries out the hair too much and can cause skin problems in dogs.)

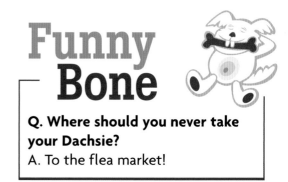

Funny Bone

Q. Where should you never take your Dachsie?
A. To the flea market!

Brush your Dachshund thoroughly before wetting his coat. For the smooth, this will remove any loose dirt from his coat. For the longhaired and wirehaired, brushing will get rid of most mats and tangles, which are more difficult to remove when the coat is wet. Make certain that your dog has a good non-slip surface on which to stand.

Begin by wetting your dog's coat. A shower or hose attachment is necessary for thoroughly wetting and rinsing the coat.

Some of the grooming tools you will need include cotton balls for ears, dog shampoo, and a brush, such as a grooming mitt.

Be sure to rinse your dog well after bathing. Soap left in the coat will make your dog itchy.

Check the water temperature to make sure that it is neither too hot nor too cold. Wet the dog with warm water, then apply the shampoo and rub it into a lather just as you do when you shampoo your own hair. Wash the head last; you do not want shampoo to drip into your dog's eyes while you are washing the rest of his body. Work the shampoo all the way down to the skin. You can use this opportunity to check the skin for any bumps, bites, or other abnormalities. Do not neglect any area of the body—get all of the hard-to-reach places.

Rinse thoroughly with warm water to remove all soap. Protect your Dachshund's eyes by shielding them with your hand and directing the flow of water in the opposite direction. You also should avoid getting water in the ear canal. Leaving a residue of chemicals can cause major harm to hair and skin, so be certain that your dog is well-rinsed. Be prepared for your dog to shake out his coat; you might want to stand back, but make sure you have a hold on him to keep him from running through the house.

Towel-dry the coat after the final rinsing. Following that, you can air-dry the coat, but you must keep your Dachsie

Did You Know? The crunchiness of unmoistened dry dog food helps keep teeth healthy by reducing plaque accumulation and massaging the gums.

out of the cold air until he is completely dry. For a quicker drying time, you may choose to use a blow dryer.

EAR CLEANING

While you're in the process of washing your Dachshund, lift each ear flap and gently wipe the inside of the ears with a damp cloth. The ears should be kept clean and any excess hair inside the ear should be carefully plucked out. Ears can be cleaned with a cotton ball and ear powder made especially for dogs. Never force your finger or any object down into the deeper part of the ear. Wipe only the surface you can see and touch easily. Any further cleaning must be performed by your vet.

Be on the lookout for any signs of infection or ear-mite infestation. If your Dachshund has been shaking his head or scratching at his ears frequently, this usually indicates a problem. If his ears have an unusual odor, this is a sure sign of mite infestation or infection, and a signal to have his ears checked by the veterinarian.

NAIL CLIPPING

Periodic nail trimming can be done during the brushing routine. Your veterinarian will teach you how to cut your dog's nails without cutting the "quick" (the blood vessels that run through the center of each nail and grow rather close to the end). The hunting Dachshund, an expert at digging, will need longer nails than his cousin who lives and plays at home.

Your Dachshund should be accustomed to having his nails trimmed at an early age because it will be part of your maintenance routine throughout his life. Not only does it look nicer, but long nails can scratch someone unintentionally. Also, a long nail has a better chance of ripping and bleeding, or causing the feet to spread. A good rule of

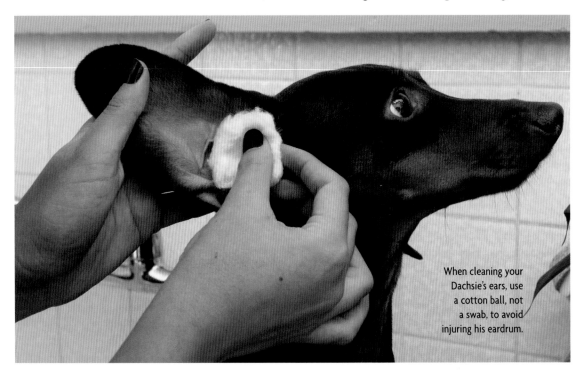

When cleaning your Dachsie's ears, use a cotton ball, not a swab, to avoid injuring his eardrum.

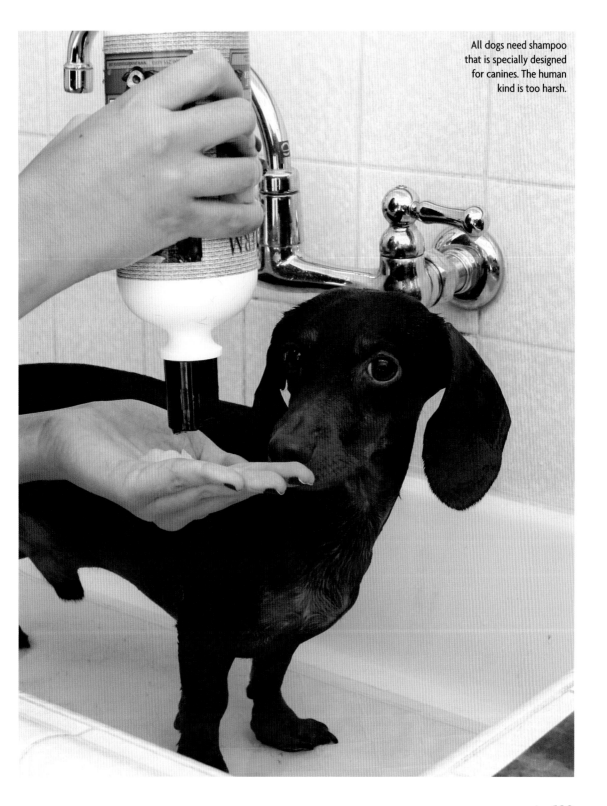

All dogs need shampoo that is specially designed for canines. The human kind is too harsh.

stop the bleeding and talk soothingly to your dog. Once he has calmed down, move on to the next nail. It is better to clip a little at a time, particularly with black-nailed dogs.

Hold your Dachsie steady as you begin trimming his nails; you do not want him to make any sudden movements or run away. Talk to him in a soothing tone and stroke him as you clip. Holding his foot in your hand, simply take off the end of each nail in one quick clip. You can purchase nail clippers that are specially made for dogs; you can find them wherever you buy grooming supplies.

There are two predominant types of clippers. One is the guillotine clipper, which is a hole with a blade in the middle. Squeeze the handles, and the blade meets the nail and chops it off. Sounds gruesome, and for some dogs, it is intolerable. Scissor-type clippers are gentler on the nail. The important thing to make sure of is that the blades on either of these clippers are sharp.

Once you are at the desired length, use a nail file to smooth the rough edges of the nails so they don't catch on carpeting or debris outdoors.

thumb is that if you can hear your dog's nails' clicking on the floor when he walks, his nails are too long.

Before you start cutting, make sure you can identify the quick in each nail. It will bleed if accidentally cut, which is painful for the dog because it contains nerve endings. Keep some type of clotting agent on hand, such as a styptic pencil or styptic powder (the type used for shaving). This will rapidly stop the bleeding when applied to the end of the cut nail. Do not panic if this happens, just

PAW PAD FUR

All Dachsie varieties need the hair between their paw pads trimmed to improve traction and minimize matting. Take a pair of straight scissors and trim the hair so it's even with the pads. While you're at it, gently handle and tug on his legs, feet, and nails. Smooths have the least amount of hair between their feet, but longhaireds and wirehaireds often have a lot of hair in between the pads.

Examine the paw pads, legs, and feet for wounds, illnesses, or other problems. For instance: Snow, ice, pebbles, thorns, and other small objects can get stuck in these areas, causing pain or injury.

DENTAL CARE

Like people, Dachshunds can suffer from dental disease, so experts recommend regular tooth brushing. Daily brushing is best, but your dog also will benefit from tooth brushing a few times a week. The teeth should be white and free of yellowish tartar, and the gums should appear healthy and pink. Gums that bleed easily when you perform dental duties may have gingivitis.

The first thing to know is that your dog probably isn't going to want your fingers in his mouth. Desensitizing your Dachshund—getting him to accept that you will be look-

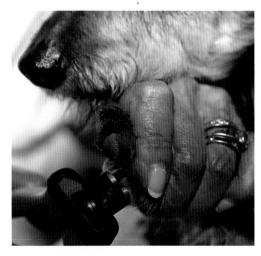

If clipping your pup's nails, do not cut the quick, which is a vein that runs through the nail.

ing at and touching his teeth—is the first step to overcoming his reticence. You can begin this with the help of the thing that motivates him most: food.

For starters, let your Dachsie lick some chicken, vegetable, or beef broth off your finger. Then, dip your finger in broth again, and gently insert your finger in the side of your dog's mouth. Touch his side teeth and gums. Several sessions will get your dog used to having his mouth touched.

Use a toothbrush that is specifically made for dogs, or a finger-tip brush wrapped around your finger, to brush your Dachsie's teeth. Hold his mouth with the fingers of one hand, and brush with the other. Use toothpaste that is made for dogs with dog-slurping flavors like poultry and beef. Human toothpaste froths too much and can give your dog an upset stomach. Brush in a circular motion with the brush held at a forty-five-degree angle to the gum line. Be sure to get the fronts, tops and sides of each tooth.

Look for signs of plaque, tartar, or gum disease, including redness, swelling, foul breath, discolored teeth, and receding gums. If you see these, take your dog to the veterinarian immediately. Also see your vet about once a year for a dental checkup.

it's a Fact

Dogs can't rinse and spit after a brushing, so dog toothpaste must be safe for pets to swallow. Always use a toothpaste specially formulated for dogs when brushing your Dachshund's teeth.

Reward-based training methods—such as clicker and luring—teach dogs what to do and help them do it correctly, setting them up for success and rewards rather than mistakes and punishment. Most dogs find food rewards meaningful; Dachshunds are no exception. In fact, they tend to be very food-motivated.

This works well for smart owners, because positive training relies on using treats, at least initially, to encourage the dog to offer a behavior. When you reinforce desired behaviors with rewards that are valuable to the dog, you are met with happy cooperation rather than resistance.

Positive does not mean permissive. While you are rewarding your Dachshund's desirable behaviors, you must manage him to be sure he doesn't get rewarded for undesirable behaviors. Training tools, such as leashes, tethers, baby gates, and crates, help keep your dog out of trouble, and the use of force-free negative punishment (the dog's behavior makes a good thing go away) helps him realize that there are negative consequences for inappropriate behaviors.

Did You Know?

The prime period for socialization is short. Most behavior experts agree that positive experiences during the ten-week period between four and fourteen weeks of age are vital to the development of a puppy that will grow into an adult dog with sound temperament.

LEARNING SOCIAL GRACES

Now that you have done all of the preparatory work and have helped your Dachsie get accustomed to his new home and family, it is time for you to have some fun! Socializing your Dachshund gives you the opportunity to show off your new friend, and your dog gets to reap the benefits of being an adorable little creature that people will want to pet and, in general, think is absolutely precious!

Besides getting to know his new family, your Dachsie should be exposed to other people, animals and situations, but of course he must not come into close contact with dogs that you don't know well until he has had all his vaccinations. This will help him become well adjusted as he grows up and less prone to being timid or fearful of the new things he will encounter.

Your Dachsie's socialization began at the breeder's home, but now it is your responsibility to continue it. The socialization he receives up until the age of twelve weeks is the most critical, as this is the time when he forms his impressions of the outside world. Be especially careful during the eight- to ten-week period, also known as the fear period. The interaction

he receives during this time should be gentle and reassuring. Lack of socialization can manifest itself in fear and aggression as the dog grows up. Your Dachsie needs lots of human contact, affection, handling, and exposure to other animals.

Once your dog has received his necessary vaccinations, feel free to take him out

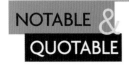

If you want to make your dog happy, create a digging spot where he's allowed to disrupt the earth. Encourage him to dig there by burying bones and toys, and helping him dig them up.

—Pat Miller, a certified pet dog trainer and owner of Peaceable Paws dog-training facility in Hagerstown, Md.

and about (on his leash, of course). Walk him around the neighborhood, take him on your daily errands, let people pet him, let him meet other dogs and pets. Make sure to expose your Dachshund to different people—men, women, kids, babies, men with beards, teenagers with cell phones or riding skateboards, joggers, shoppers, someone in a wheelchair, a pregnant woman, etc. Make sure your Dachshund explores different surfaces like sidewalks, gravel, a puddle. Positive experience is the key to building confidence. It's up to you make sure your Dachshund safely discovers the world so he will be a calm, confident, and well-socialized dog.

It's very important that you take the lead in all socialization experiences and never put your Dachsie into a scary or potentially harmful situation. Be mindful of your dog's

SMART TIP! **If your Dachsie refuses to sit** with both haunches squarely beneath him and instead sits on one side or the other, he may have a physical reason for doing so. Discuss the habit with your veterinarian to be certain that your dog isn't suffering from some structural problem.

limitations. Fifteen minutes at a public market is fine; two hours at a loud outdoor concert is probably too much. Meeting vaccinated, tolerant, and gentle older dogs is great. Meeting dogs that you don't know isn't such a great idea, especially if they appear very energetic, dominant, or fearful. Control the situations in which you place your dog.

Teaching your Dachsie the stay (pictured) and down cues (opposite page) is vital to keeping him safe outdoors.

One way to get your dog's attention is to lure him into position with a small treat.

The best way to socialize your Dachsie to a new experience is to make him think it's the best thing ever. You can do this with a lot of happy talk, enthusiasm, and, yes, food.

To convince your dog that almost any experience is a blast, always carry treats. Consider carrying two types—a bag of his puppy kibble, which you can give him when introducing him to nonthreatening experiences, and a bag of high-value, mouthwatering treats to give him when introducing him to scarier experiences.

Chanel, a twenty-year-old wirehaired Dachshund from Port Jefferson Station, N.Y., is listed as the world's oldest known dog in the 2010 edition of *Guinness World Records*.

BASIC CUES

All Dachshunds, regardless of your training and relationship goals, need to know at least five basic behaviors: sit, down, stay, come, and heel. Here are tips for teaching your dog these important cues.

Sit: Every dog should learn how to sit on command.

■ Hold a treat at the end of your Dachshund's nose.

■ Move the treat over his head.

■ When your Dachsie sits, click a clicker or say "yes!"

■ Feed your dog the treat.

■ If your Dachsie jumps up, hold the treat lower. If he backs up, back him into a corner and wait until he sits. Be patient. Keep your clicker handy, and click (or say "yes!") and treat anytime he offers a sit.

■ When he offers sits easily, say "sit" just before he offers, so he can make the association between the word and the behavior.

Add the sit cue when you know you can get the behavior. Your dog doesn't know what the word means until you repeatedly associate it with the appropriate behavior.

■ When your Dachshund sits easily on cue, start using intermittent reinforcement by clicking some sits but not others. At first, click most sits and skip an occasional one (this is a high rate of reinforcement). Gradually make your clicks more and more random.

Down: If your dog can sit, he can lie down, and "down" is one of the easiest commands for Dachshunds because they exist in a nearly prone position.

▲ Have your dog sit.

▲ Hold the treat in front of his nose.

▲ Move it down slowly, straight toward the floor (toward his toes). If he follows all the way down, click and treat.

▲ If he gets stuck, move the treat down more slowly. Click and treat for small movements downward—moving his head a bit lower, or inching one paw forward. Keep clicking and treating until he is all the way down. This is called "shaping"—rewarding small pieces of a behavior until your dog succeeds.

▲ If he stands as you move the treat toward the floor, have him sit, and move the treat more slowly downward, shaping with clicks and treats for small movement down as long as he is sitting. If he stands, cheerfully say "Oops!" (which means "Sorry, no treat for that!"), have him sit, and try again.

▲ If shaping isn't working, sit on the floor with your knee raised. Have your Dachsie sit next to you. Put your hand with the treat under your knee and lure him under your leg so that he lies down and crawls to follow the treat. Click and treat!

▲ When you can lure the down easily, add the verbal cue, wait a few seconds to let your dog think, then lure him down to show him the association. Repeat until he'll go down on the verbal cue. Then begin using intermittent reinforcement.

Stay: What good are the sit and down cues if your dog doesn't stay?

● Start with your Dachshund in a sit or down position.

● Put the treat in front of his nose and keep it there.

● Click and reward several times while he is in position, then release him with a cue that you will always use to tell him the stay is over. Common release cues are: "all done," "break," "free," "free dog," "at ease," and "OK."

● When your dog will stay in a sit or down position while you click and treat, add your verbal stay cue. Say "stay," pause for a second or two, click and say "stay" again. Then release your dog.

● When he's getting the idea, say "stay," whisk the treat out of sight behind your back, click and whisk the treat back. Be sure to get it all the way to his nose, so he doesn't jump up. Gradually increase the duration of the stay.

● When your dog will stay for fifteen to twenty seconds, add small distractions: shuffling your feet, moving your arms, small hops. Increase distractions very gradually. If he makes mistakes, you're adding too much too fast.

● When he'll stay for fifteen to twenty seconds with distractions, gradually add distance. Have your dog stay, take a half-step back, click, return, and treat. When he'll stay with a half-step, tell him to stay, take a full step back, click, and return. Always return to

it's a Fact

The official mascot of the 1972 Summer Olympics in Munich, Germany, was a Dachshund named Waldi! The hound represented what all athletes needed to have: resistance, tenacity, and agility.

your dog to treat after you click, but before you release. If you always return, his stay becomes strong. If you call him to you, his stay gets weaker due to his eagerness to come to you.

Come: A reliable recall—coming when called—can be a challenging behavior to teach. It is possible, however. To succeed, you need to install an automatic response to your come cue—one so automatic that your Dachsie doesn't even stop to think when he hears it, but will spin on his heels and charge to you at full speed.

◆ Start by charging a come cue the same way you charged your clicker. If your Dachshund already ignores the word "come," pick a different cue, like "front" or "hugs." Say your cue and feed him a bit of scrumptious treat, like boiled chicken. Repeat this until his eyes light up when he hears the cue. Now you're ready to start training.

◆ With your dog on a leash, run away several steps and cheerfully call out your charged cue. When he follows, click the clicker. Feed him a treat when he reaches you. For a more enthusiastic come, run away at full speed as you call him. When he follows at a gallop, click, stop running and give him a treat. The better your dog gets at coming, the farther away he can be when you call him.

◆ Once your dog understands the come cue, play with more people, each with a clicker and treats. Stand a short distance apart and take turns calling and running away. Click and treat in turn as he comes to each of you. Gradually increase the distance until he comes flying to each person from a distance.

◆ When you're ready to practice in wide-open spaces, attach a long line—a 20- to 50-foot leash—so you can gather him up if that squirrel is too much of a tempta-

SMART TIP!

If you begin teaching the heel cue by taking long walks and letting your dog pull you along, he may misinterpret this action as an acceptable form of taking a walk. When you pull back on the leash to counteract his pulling, he will read that tug as a signal to pull even harder!

Though they are small and can be easily carried, Dachsies should be allowed to see the world on their own four paws.

Teaching new cues requires patience on the owner's part.

tion. Then go practice where there are less tempting distractions.

Heel: Heeling means that your Dachshund walks beside you without pulling. It takes time and patience on the owner's part to succeed at teaching the dog that he (the owner) will not proceed unless the

SMART TIP!

Once your Dachsie understands what behavior goes with a specific cue, start weaning him off the food treats. At first, give a treat after each exercise. Then, start to give a treat only after every other exercise. Mix up the times when you offer a food reward and the times when you only offer praise so that your dog will never know when he is going to receive both food and praise and when he is going to receive only praise.

dog is walking calmly beside him. Pulling out ahead on the leash is definitely not acceptable dog behavior.

▼ Begin by holding the leash in your left hand as your Dachshund sits beside your left leg. Move the loop end of the leash to your right hand but keep your left hand short on the leash so that it keeps your dog close to you.

▼ Say "heel" and step forward on your left foot. Keep your dog close to you and take three steps. Stop and have him sit next to you in what we now call the heel position. Praise verbally, but do not touch him. Hesitate a moment and begin again with "heel," taking three steps and stopping, at which point your dog is told to sit again.

▼ Your goal here is to have your Dachsie walk those three steps without pulling on the leash. Once he will walk calmly beside you for three steps without pulling, increase

 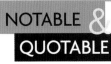
It's not difficult to socialize Dachshunds. After all, they wouldn't be in the top ten most popular breeds if they didn't make great pets. People seem to like having a dog with some independence. Respect that independence. It can be endearing if you channel it in the right direction.

—Lisa Warren, a Dachshund breeder and trainer

the number of steps you take to five. When he will walk politely beside you while you take five steps, increase the length of your walk to ten steps. Keep increasing the length of your stroll until your dog will walk quietly beside you without pulling as long as you want him to heel. When you stop heeling, indicate to him that the exercise is over by verbally praising as you pet him and say "OK, good dog." The "OK" is used as a release word, meaning that the exercise is finished and he is free to relax.

▼ If you are dealing with a dog that insists on pulling, simply "put on your brakes" and stand your ground until he realizes that the two of you are not going anywhere until he is beside you and moving at your pace. It may take some time just standing there to convince the dog that you are the leader and you will be the one to decide on the direction and speed of your travel.

▼ Each time your Dachsie looks up at you or slows down to give a slack leash between the two of you, quietly praise him and say, "Good heel. Good dog." Eventually, your dog will begin to respond and within a few days he will be walking politely beside you without pulling on the leash. At first, the training sessions should be kept short and positive; soon he will be able to walk nicely with you for increasingly longer distances. Remember also to give your Dachsie free time and the opportunity to run and play when you have finished heel practice.

TRAINING TIPS

If not properly socialized, managed, and trained, even well-bred Dachshunds will exhibit undesirable behaviors such as jumping up, barking, chasing, chewing and other destructive behaviors. Prevent these annoying habits and help your Dachsie become the perfect dog you're hoping for by following some basic training and behavior tenets.

✔ **Be consistent.** Consistency is important, not just in relation to what you allow your dog to do (get on the sofa, perhaps) and not do (jump up on people) but also in the verbal and body language cues you use with your dog and in his daily routine.

✔ **Be gentle but firm.** Positive training methods are becoming the norm. Dog-friendly methods, properly applied, are wonderfully effective, creating canine–human relationships based on mutual respect and cooperation.

✔ **Manage behavior.** All living things repeat behaviors that reward them. Behaviors that aren't reinforced will go away.

✔ **Provide adequate exercise.** A tired dog is a well-behaved dog. Many behavioral problems can be avoided, others resolved, simply by providing your dog with enough exercise.

THE THREE-STEP PROGRAM

Perhaps it's too late to give your dog consistency, training, and management from the start. Maybe he came from a Dachshund rescue or a shelter, or you didn't realize the importance of these tenets when he was a pup. He already may have learned some bad behaviors. Perhaps they're even part of his genetic package. Many unwanted behaviors can be modified with relative ease using the following three-step process for changing an unwanted behavior.

STEP 1: Visualize the behavior you want. If you simply try to stop your dog from doing something, you leave a behavior vacuum.

SMART TIP!

It is a good idea to enroll in an obedience class in your area. Many pet-supply stores have dog clubs offer basic obedience training as well as preparatory classes for obedience competition. There are also local dog trainers who offer similar classes.

You need to fill that vacuum with something, so your dog doesn't return to the same behavior or fill it with one even worse! If you're tired of your dog jumping up, decide what you'd prefer instead. A dog that greets people by sitting politely in front of them is a joy to own.

STEP 2: Prevent your dog from being rewarded for the behavior you don't want. Management to the rescue! When your Dachsie jumps up to greet you or get your attention, turn your back and step away to show him that jumping up no longer works to gain attention. Step through a door, if necessary.

STEP 3: Generously reinforce the desired behavior. Remember, dogs repeat behaviors that reward them. If your Dachshund no longer gets attention for jumping up and is heavily reinforced with attention and treats for sitting, he will offer sits instead of jumping because sits get him what he wants.

COUNTER CONDITIONING

Behaviors that respond well to the three-step process are those where the dog does something in order to get good stuff. He jumps up to get attention. He nips at your hands to get you to play with him.

The three steps don't work well when you're dealing with behaviors that are based in strong emotion, such as aggression and fear, or with hardwired behaviors such as chasing prey. With these, you can change the emotional response through counter conditioning—programming a new emotional or automatic response to the stimulus by giving it a new association. Here's how you would counter condition your dog who chases after skateboarders when you're walking him.

● Have a large supply of very high-value treats, such as canned chicken.

● Station yourself with your Dachsie on a leash at a location where skateboarders will pass by at a subthreshold distance "X"—that is, where he alerts but doesn't lunge.

● Wait for a skateboarder. The instant your dog notices the skateboarder, feed him bits of chicken, nonstop, until the skateboard is gone. Then stop feeding him the chicken.

● Repeat until, when the skateboarder appears, your Dachsie looks at you as if to say, "Yay! Where's my chicken?" This is a conditioned emotional response, or CER.

● When you have a consistent CER at X, decrease the distance slightly, perhaps minus one foot, and repeat until you consistently get the CER at this distance.

● Continue decreasing the distance and obtaining a CER at each level, until a skateboarder zooming right past your Dachsie elicits the happy "Where's my chicken?" CER. Now go back to distance X and add a second skateboarder. Continue this process of gradual desensitization until your Dachsie doesn't turn a hair at a bevy of skateboarders.

Discipline—training one to act in accordance with rules—brings order to life. It is as simple as that. Without discipline, particularly in a group society, chaos reigns supreme, and the group will eventually perish. Humans and canines are social animals and need some form of discipline to function effectively. Dogs need discipline in their lives in order to understand how their pack (you and other family members) functions, and how they must act in order to survive.

The following behavioral problems are the ones which owners most commonly encounter. Every dog is unique and every situation is unique. Because behavioral abnormalities are the leading reason for owners' abandoning their pets, we hope that you will make a valiant effort to solve your Dachshund's problems.

NIP NIPPING

As puppies start to teethe, they feel the need to sink their teeth into anything—

Did You Know?

Anxiety can make a dog really miserable. Living in a world with vaporous monsters and suspected Dachshund-eaters roaming the streets has to be nerve-wracking. The good news is that dogs are not doomed to be forever ruled by fear. Smart owners who understand the timid Dachsie's needs can help him build self-confidence and a more optimistic view of life.

unfortunately, that includes your fingers, arms, hair, toes, whatever happens to be available. You may find this behavior cute for about the first five seconds—until you feel just how sharp those puppy teeth are. This is something you want to discourage immediately and consistently with a firm "No!" (or whatever number of firm "Nos" it takes for your Dachsie to understand that you mean business). Replace your finger with an appropriate chew toy.

STOP THAT WHINING

A puppy will often cry, whine, whimper, howl, or make some type of commotion when he is left alone. This is basically his way of calling out for attention, of calling out to make sure that you know he is there and that you have not forgotten about him. He feels insecure when he is left alone; for example, when you are out of the house and he is in his crate, or when you are in another part of the house and he cannot see you. The noise he is making is an expression of the anxiety he feels at being alone, so he needs to be taught that being alone is OK. You are not actually training the dog to stop making noise; you are training him to feel comfortable when he is alone and removing the need to make the noise.

This is where the crate with a cozy blanket and a toy comes in handy. You want to know that your pup is safe when you are not there to supervise, and you know that he will be safe in his crate rather than

roaming freely about the house. In order for the pup to stay in his crate without making a fuss, he needs to be comfortable in his crate. On that note, it is extremely important that the crate is never used as a form of punishment, or the pup will have a negative association with the crate.

Accustom your Dachshund to the crate in short, gradually increasing intervals of time in which you put him in the crate, maybe with a treat, and stay in the room with him. If he cries or makes a fuss, do not go to him, but stay in his sight. Gradually,

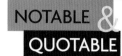

Dachsies are fun dogs and need to be able to be themselves. However, they will run all over you if you let them. They need rules. You need to be firm with them because if you let them have a little bit of slack, they will want more. Smart dogs need to be challenged.

—Becky Burguess, Dachshund breeder, from Power, Mont.

he will realize that staying in his crate is all right, and it will not be so traumatic for him when you are not around. You may want to leave the radio on softly when you leave the house; the sound of human voices can be comforting to him.

CHEW ON THIS

The national canine pastime is chewing! Every dog loves to sink his "canines" into a tasty bone, but most anything will do! Dogs need to chew to massage their gums, to make their new teeth feel better, and to exercise their jaws. This is a natural behavior deeply imbedded in all things canine. Our role as smart owners is not to stop chewing, but to redirect it to positive, chew-worthy objects. Be an informed owner and purchase proper chew toys for your Dachshund, like strong nylon bones. Be sure that the devices are safe and durable because your dog's safety is at risk.

SMART TIP!

The golden rule of dog training is simple. For each "question" (command), there is only one correct answer (reaction). One command equals one reaction. Keep practicing the command until the dog reacts correctly without hesitation. Be repetitive but not monotonous. Dogs get bored just as people do; a bored dog's attention will not be focused on the lesson.

The best way to redirect chewing is prevention: That is, put your shoes, handbags, and other tasty objects in their proper places (out of the reach of the growing canine mouth). Direct dogs to their toys whenever you see them tasting the furniture legs or the leg of your pants. Make a loud noise to attract the dog's attention, and immediately escort him to his chew toy and engage him with the toy for at least four minutes, praising and encouraging him all the while.

Escapes can be halted by making sure your fence is secure and does not have holes big enough for your dog to squeeze through.

NO MORE JUMPING

Jumping up is a dog's friendly way of saying hello, and some energetic Dachshunds may get in this habit. Some dog owners do not mind when their dog jumps up, which is fine for them, but Dachsie owners should discourage this for many reasons. The problem arises when guests come to the house and the dog greets them in the same manner—whether they like it or not! However friendly the greeting may be, chances are your visitors will not appreciate nearly being knocked over. The dog will not be able to distinguish upon whom he can jump and whom he cannot. Remember: The Dachshund's long

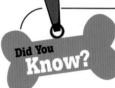

Did You Know?

Some natural remedies for separation anxiety are reputed to have calming effects, but check with your vet before using them. Flower essence remedies, first developed by Dr. Edward Bach, are water-based extracts of plants, which are stabilized and preserved with brandy. A human dose is only a few drops, so seek advice from a natural healing practitioner about proper dosage.

Your Dachshund may howl, whine, or otherwise vocalize his displeasure at your leaving the house and his being left alone. This is a normal case of separation anxiety, but there are things that can be done to eliminate this problem. Your dog needs to learn that he will be fine on his own for a while and that he will not wither away if he isn't attended to every minute of the day.

In fact, constant attention can lead to separation anxiety in the first place. If you are endlessly coddling and cuddling your dog, he will come to expect this from you all of the time and it will be more traumatic for him when you are not there.

One thing you can do to minimize separation anxiety is to make your entrances and exits as low-key as possible. Do not give your dog a long drawn-out goodbye, and do not lavish him with hugs and kisses when you return. This is giving in to the attention that he craves, and it will only make him miss it more when you are away.

Another thing you can try is to give your dog a treat when you leave; this will keep him occupied *and* keep his mind off the fact that you just left. It also will help him associate your leaving with a pleasant experience.

You may have to accustom your dog to being left alone in intervals, much like when you introduced your pup to his crate. Of course, when your dog starts whimpering as you approach the door, your first instinct will be to run to him and comfort him, but don't do it! Eventually he will adjust and be just fine if you take it in small steps.

His anxiety stems from being placed in an unfamiliar situation; by familiarizing him with being alone he will learn that he is OK. That is not to say you should purposely leave your dog home alone, but the dog needs to know that while he can depend on you for his care, you do not have to be by his side 24 hours a day.

Supervise your dog when he's outside to stop him from tearing up your garden.

back was not designed for vertical greetings; too much jumping up can stress your hot dog's back. Therefore, it is surely best to discourage this behavior entirely from a young age.

Pick a command such as "Off!" (avoid using "down" because you will use that for the dog to lie down) and tell him "Off!" when he jumps up. Place him on the ground on all fours and have him sit, praising him the whole time. Always lavish him with praise and petting when he is in the "sit" position. That way you are still giving him a warm, affectionate greeting, because you are as excited to see him as he is to see you!

CAN YOU DIG IT?

Digging, which is seen as a destructive behavior to humans, is an extremely natural behavior in earthdogs like Dachshunds. Telling a Dachsie not to dig is like tell you not to breathe! Your wiener lives to dig and his desire to disturb terra firma can be irrepressible and most frustrating to his owners. When digging occurs in your yard, it is actually a normal behavior redirected into something

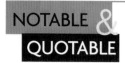

NOTABLE & QUOTABLE

Stage false departures. Pick up your car keys and put on your coat, then put them away and go about your routine. Do this several times a day, ignoring your dog while you do it. Soon his reaction to these triggers will decrease.

— *September Morn, a dog trainer and behavior specialist in Bellingham, Wash.*

the dog can do in his everyday life. Who are you to say that a badger or rabbit didn't visited that clump or earth six hours prior? Your Dachshund's nose knows, and his paws will get to the bottom of it.

Beyond these strong instincts, your dog is digging as a reaction to boredom. It is somewhat similar to someone eating a whole bag of chips in front of the television, because

SMART TIP!

Do not carry your dog to his relief area. Lead him there on a leash or, better yet, encourage him to follow you to the spot. If you start carrying him, you might end up doing this routine forever, and your dog will have the satisfaction of having trained you.

Dachsie pups should not be allowed access to steps, which could injure their fragile spines.

they are there! Dachshunds love a job and live to please their owners by doing it well—well, most Dachshunds do. Always provide your busy earthdog with adequate play and exercise so that his mind and paws are occupied, and so that he feels that he is doing something useful. Think about earthdog events or any of the other performance events that Dachsies excel in.

Finally, digging is easiest to control if it is stopped as soon as possible. It is often hard to catch a dog in the act, though you may catch your Dachsie two feet into his new tunnel! One solution is to designate an area on your property where it is OK for him to dig. If you catch him digging in an off-limits area of the yard, immediately bring him to the approved area and praise him for digging there. Keep a close eye on him so that you can catch him.

Diligence is needed from a dog owner to curb unwanted actions.

UNWANTED BARKING MUST GO

Barking is a dog's way of talking, and hounds like Dachshunds always seem to have something to say. It can be somewhat frustrating because it is not easy to tell what a dog means by his bark: is he excited, happy, frightened, angry? Whatever it is that the dog is trying to say, he should not be punished for barking. It is only when the barking becomes excessive, and when the excessive barking becomes a bad habit, that the behavior needs to be modified.

If an intruder came into your home in the middle of the night and the dog barked a warning, wouldn't you be pleased? You would probably deem your dog a hero, a wonderful guardian, and protector of the home. On the other hand, if a friend drops by unexpectedly and rings the doorbell and is greeted with a sudden sharp bark, you would probably be annoyed at the dog. But isn't it just the same behavior? The dog doesn't know any better—unless he sees who is at the door and it is someone he is familiar with, he will bark as a means of vocalizing that his (and your) territory is being threatened. While your friend is not posing a threat, it is all the same to the dog. Barking is his way of letting you know that there is an intrusion, whether friend or foe, on your property. This type of barking is instinctive and should not be discouraged.

Excessive habitual barking, however, is a problem that should be corrected early on. As your Dachshund grows up, you will be able to tell when his barking is purposeful and when it is for no reason. You will become able to distinguish your dog's different barks and with what they are associated. For example, the bark when someone comes to the door will be different from the bark when he is excited to see you. It is similar to a person's tone of voice, except that the dog has to rely totally on tone of voice because he does not have the benefit of using words. An incessant barker will be evident at an early age.

There are some things that encourage a dog to bark. For example, if your dog barks nonstop for a few minutes and you give him a treat to quiet him, he believes that you are rewarding him for barking. He will associate barking with getting a treat, and will keep doing it until he is rewarded.

STOP FOOD STEALING AND BEGGING

Is your dog devising ways of stealing food from your cupboards? If so, you must answer the following questions: Is your Dachshund hungry, or is just like every other chowhound wondering why there is food on the coffee table? Face it, some dogs are more food-motivated than others; some dogs are totally obsessed by a slab of brisket and can only think of their next meal. Food stealing is terrific fun and always yields a great reward—food, glorious food!

The smart owner's goal, therefore, is to make the "reward" less rewarding, even startling! Plant a shaker can (an empty can with coins inside) on the table so that it catches your pooch off-guard. There are other devices available that will surprise the dog when he is looking for a mid-afternoon snack. Such remote-control devices, though not the first choice of some trainers, allow

When teaching your Dachsie what not to do, keep the lessons short and sweet.

the correction to come from the object instead of the owner. These devices are also useful to keep the snacking hound from napping on furniture that is forbidden.

Just like food stealing, begging is a favorite pastime of hungry puppies with that same reward—food! No dog looks as desperate and appealing as a Dachshund standing on his hind legs! Dogs quickly learn that humans love that pose and may be willing to share the "good food" with their Dachsies. Begging is a conditioned response related to a specific stimulus, time, and place. The sounds of the kitchen—cans and bottles opening, crin-

kling bags—and the smell of food in preparation will excite the chowhound and soon the paws are in the air!

Here is the solution to stopping this behavior: Never give in to a beggar, no matter how appealing or desperate! You are rewarding the dog for sitting pretty, jumping up, whining, and rubbing his nose into you by giving him that glorious reward—food. By ignoring the dog, you will (eventually) force the behavior into extinction. Note that the behavior likely gets worse before it disappears, so be sure there aren't any "softies" in the family who will give in to your dog every time he whimpers, "More, please."

POOP ALERT!

Feces eating, aka coprophagia, is, to most humans, one of the most disgusting behaviors that a dog could engage in, yet to the dog it is perfectly normal. Vets have found that diets with a low digestibility, containing relatively low levels of fiber and high levels of starch, increase coprophagia. Therefore, high-fiber diets may decrease the likelihood of dogs eating feces. To discourage this behavior, feed food that is nutritionally complete and in the proper amount. If changes in his diet do not seem to work, and no medical cause can be found, you will have to modify the behavior through environmental control before it becomes a habit.

There are some tricks you can try, such as adding an unpleasant-tasting substance to the feces to make them unpalatable or adding something to the dog's food which will make it unpleasant tasting after it passes through the dog. The best way to

SMART TIP!

Do not have long practice sessions with your Dachshund. He will become easily bored if you do. Also, never practice when you are tired, ill, worried, or in a negative mood. This will transmit to your Dachsie and may have an adverse effect on his performance.

prevent your dog from eating his stool is to make it unavailable—clean up after he eliminates and remove any stool from the yard. If it is not there, he cannot eat it.

Never reprimand the dog for stool eating, as this rarely impresses the dog. Vets recommend distracting the dog while he is in the act of stool eating. Another option is to muzzle the dog when he is in the yard to relieve himself; this usually is effective within thirty to sixty days. Coprophagia most frequently is seen in pups six to twelve months of age, and usually disappears around the dog's first birthday.

If you stay on top of your dog's bad behavior, it will usually disappear with time.

Dachshunds are hardy little dogs, capable of running down badgers and hares and burrowing into tunnels with great endurance. However, most Dachshunds live much quieter lives, with their exercise limited to what they do with their owners and families. How they must miss the excitement of chasing a badger down a hole!

It would not be wise to let your Dachshund sit home alone all week while you are at work, and then try to exercise him in the great outdoors on the weekend. To enjoy and benefit from physical exercise, dogs must enjoy that exercise on a regular basis. One day a week is insufficient to create a fit Dachsie—or human!

Walking is just as beneficial for dogs as it is for humans. Thus, a brisk walk of a reasonable distance is still the best possible way to exercise lungs and limbs. Moreover, the human walker also will reap the benefits of regular exercise.

it's a **Fact**

The Fédération Internationale Cynologique is the world kennel club that governs dog shows in Europe and elsewhere around the world. At every FCI dog shows, Dachshunds always win their group! This is possible because Group 4 contains no other breed except Dachshunds!

Before You Begin
Because of the physical demands of sporting activities, a Dachshund puppy shouldn't begin officially training until he is done growing. That doesn't mean, though, that you can't begin socializing him to sports. Talk to your vet about what age is appropriate.

Fetching games in which the dog runs after items such as a ball or Frisbee are also excellent ways to exercise. As you begin teaching your Dachsie to fetch, remember that he's a predator at heart, and he instinctively loves to chase things. A ball, to him, is just as exciting as a rabbit, providing that it's moving and he can catch it. Be sure to praise lavishly when he does, so he will be anxious to do it again and again.

In case you mistakenly thought your lap-warming Dachshund is just a pet, take note: The Dachshund's underground persona may be quite unlike what you see above ground. Think of your Dachsie as a hound with an attitude. This breed is active in den trials (below-ground hunting; also known as earthdog or go-to-ground trials), field trials (above-ground hunting), tracking, obedience, agility, rally, and conformation.

EARTHDOG TESTS

When it comes to doing what comes naturally, earthdog events are at the top of the list for Dachshunds because they were bred to "go to ground," which is to hunt prey that hides in burrows. Earthdog events test a dog's willingness to follow the scent of prey, enter a burrow, and "work the quarry."

According to American Kennel Club rules, Dachshunds must be six months of age to participate in the tests and can compete at four class levels: Introduction to Quarry, Junior Earthdog, Senior Earthdog, and Master Earthdog. Artificial or live quarry is

Earthdog (pictured here and opposite page) allows your hound to harness his superb sense of smell.

used in these tests, though cages protect the rats from physical (if not psychological) harm. The stated purpose of earthdog tests is to provide the dogs the chance to demonstrate their natural talent in following and pursuing game.

Earthdog events begin with the Introduction to Quarry. In this event, small terriers and Dachsies must negotiate a ten-foot-long underground tunnel with a right angle turn. A cage containing rats is at the end of the tunnel, with a set of bars in front of it. The dog is expected to go into the tunnel and try to get at the rats.

Dogs who pass this initial test can go on to earn the earthdog titles of Junior Earthdog, Senior Earthdog, and Master Earth-

dog. Each of these levels of earthdog testing becomes more challenging, with tunnel lengths getting longer and time elements added. Ultimately, the goal is the same: the dog must negotiate the tunnel and work the quarry.

If you're interested in getting involved in earthdog work, contact the American Working Terrier Association or the AKC for dates, times, and locations of upcoming events in your area. Watching an earthdog test firsthand and talking with owners will give you a good overview of the sport. If you bring your Dachshund, you often will be able to practice with your dog and a judge or experienced club member after the tests are completed for the day. Or, you might just want to enter the entry-level test on the spot.

In addition, check to see if there is a local terrier or Dachshund club in your area with members who participate in earthdog work. Often, clubs have a site with permanent dens for club members to practice with their dogs.

If you're interested in introducing your Dachshund to the sport of den tests, the unanimous sentiment from experienced trialers is, "Go for it!" Both dogs and smart owners can enjoy this sport. Testing in earthdog work is relatively inexpensive. Earth trials usually take place on weekends, so you can't use, "I've got to work," as an excuse. Even though places are awarded in AWTA trials, earthdog tests are considered noncompetitive in that the dog only needs to receive a passing score to achieve his title. In other words, a dog doesn't have to beat the times of other dogs to earn points toward a title.

As a result of this noncompetitive nature, earthdog work attracts a variety of Dachshunds and owners, representing a diversity of backgrounds and a range of ages. Women make up as much as half of the owner entries, and husband-and-wife teams also are very common. No hunting skills are required on your part (professional trainers and handlers are virtually nonexistent in this sport), and little to no training is required of the dogs.

FIELD TRIALS

Field trials are offered to the retrievers, pointers, and spaniel breeds of the Sporting Group as well as to the Beagles, Dachshunds, and Bassets of the Hound Group. The purpose of field trials is to demonstrate a dog's ability to perform his original purpose in the field. The events vary depending on the type of dog, but in all trials dogs compete against one another for placement and for points toward their Field Champion titles.

Dachsies can be very active, but they also can relax with the best of them!

Dachshunds participate in trials similar to those used for Beagles and Basset Hounds. The main purpose of the trial is to trail a rabbit, whether in a brace (a pair) or in small groups. The trial is judged based on the Dachshund's accuracy in following its quarry.

To get a sense of whether your Dachshund will enjoy field trial work, take him to an area where you normally see lots of rabbits and get him started. Dusk is the best time of day for this because that's when rabbits come out to feed. Keep your eyes open for a rabbit, and once you see one, notice the path it takes when it goes into the bushes. Take your dog to the spot where the rabbit had been feeding and encourage him to sniff the ground. If you see him pick up the scent, tell him he's a good boy. His interest in following the rabbit's scent indicates he has the instinct needed to compete in field trials.

TRACKING

Any dog is capable of tracking, using his nose to follow a trail. The Dachshund's superb scenting ability and low-to-the-ground stature make him ideally suited for tracking tests. The AKC started tracking tests in 1937, when the first licensed test took place as part of the Utility level at an obedience trial.

Ten years later, in 1947, the AKC offered the first title, Tracking Dog. It was not until 1980 that the AKC added the Tracking Dog Excellent title, which was followed by the Versatile Surface Tracking title in 1995. The title Champion Tracker is awarded to a dog who has earned all three titles.

Your Dachshund must be at least six months old to participate in a tracking trial, but you can get started teaching him this sport by encouraging him to find objects

SMART TIP!

Contain your Dachshund's digging instincts by building her a badger den. Make a small sandbox and fill it with warm, inviting earth.

using scent. You can start with treats and work up to other objects. Get help by joining a tracking class, which will get you started on the right path to training your dog.

OBEDIENCE TRIALS

Obedience trials in the United States trace back to the early 1930s, when organized obedience training was developed to demonstrate how well dog and owner could work together. The pioneer of obedience trials is Mrs. Helen Whitehouse Walker, a Standard Poodle fancier, who designed a series of exercises after the Associated Sheep, Police Army Dog Society of Great Britain. Since the days of Mrs. Walker, obedience trials have grown by leaps and bounds, and today there are over 2,000 trials held in the United States every year, with more than 100,000 dogs competing. Any registered AKC or ILP (Indefinite Listing Privilege) dog can enter an obedience trial, regardless of conformational disqualifications or neutering.

Obedience trials are divided into three levels of progressive difficulty. At the first level, the Novice, dogs compete for the title Companion Dog; at the intermediate level, the Open, dogs compete for the title Companion Dog Excellent; and at the advanced level, dogs compete for the title Utility Dog. Classes are subdivided into "A" (for beginners) and "B" (for more experienced handlers). A perfect score at any level is 200, and a dog must score 170 or better to earn a "leg," of which three are needed to earn the title. To earn points, the dog must

score more than fifty percent of the available points in each exercise; the possible points range from twenty to forty.

Once a dog has earned the UD title, he can compete with other proven obedience dogs for the coveted title of Utility Dog Excellent, which requires that the dog win "legs" in ten shows. In 1977, the title Obedience Trial Champion was established by the AKC. Utility Dogs who earn "legs" in Open B and Utility B earn points toward their Obedience Trial Champion title. To become an OTCh., a dog needs to earn 100 points, which requires three first places in Open B and Utility under three different judges.

it's a Fact

The Dachshund is the only hound allowed to enter the American Kennel Club's terrier earthdog events because he is the only hound who was bred to follow quarry underground.

The Grand Prix of obedience trials, the AKC National Obedience Invitational, gives qualifying Utility Dogs the chance to win the newest and highest title: National Obedience Champion. Only the top 25 ranked obedience dogs, plus any dog ranked in the top three in his breed, are allowed to compete.

AGILITY TRIALS

Agility is one of the most popular dog sports out there. Dachshunds are excellent at this activity, which requires speed, precision, and obedience. Training your Dachshund in agility will boost his confidence and teach him to focus on you.

At dog shows, judges examine dogs to see how well they conform to the written standard for that breed.

In agility competition, the dog and handler move through a prescribed course, negotiating a series of obstacles that may include jumps, tunnels, dog walk, A-frame, seesaw, pause table, and weave poles. Dogs that run through a course without refusing any obstacles, going off course or knocking down any bars, all within a set time, get a qualifying score. Dogs with a certain number of qualifying scores in their given division (Novice, Open, Excellent, and Mach, at AKC trials) earn an agility title.

Several different organizations recognize agility events. AKC-sanctioned agility events are the most common. The United States Dog Agility Association also sanctions agility trials, as does the United Kennel Club. The rules are different for each of these organizations, but the principles are the same.

When Dachshunds compete in agility, they usually jump at a height of only 4 or 8 inches, depending on the height of the dog. With the exception of the jumps, Dachshunds are expected to negotiate the other obstacles on the course at the same height and distance as other breeds (the one exception is the pause table, which is lowered). Because each division of agility is subdivided by jump height, Dachshunds compete for ribbons against other dogs their own size.

When your Dachshund starts his agility training, he will begin by learning to negotiate each individual obstacle while on-leash, as you guide him. Eventually, you will steer him through a few obstacles in a row, one after another. Once he catches on that this is how agility works, he can run a short course off-leash. One day, you'll see the light go on in his eyes as he figures out that he should look to you for guidance as he runs through a course. Your job will be to tell him which obstacles to take next, using your voice and your body as signals.

True Tails

Six years ago, after losing my wirehaired Dachshund Willie to cancer, I never dreamed I could love another dog as much. Not only did the new dog, Auggie, fill the void, but he has taken me on a journey I never even imagined.

The breeder placed Auggie with us as a pet, thinking he showed little desire for hunting or tracking. When he was six months old, while on a walk, he saw a rabbit and began to voice. Voicing is a highly desirable trait for Dachshunds: It is a sound similar to a guttural bark and proclaims that the dog has found a scent.

The world of Dachshunds and all they were bred to do opened up for Auggie and me. We were introduced to earthdog trials, conformation shows, and obedience. Our main interest was participating in the working/hunting events. Because Auggie's breeder breeds Dachshunds for tracking wounded game, we utilized these methods to train Auggie.

We competed in earthdog trials, and Auggie earned his Junior, Senior, and Master Earthdog titles. We had so much fun together, my hobby turned into a passion. We trained for and achieved some German titles as well, in gun shyness and field obedience.

Auggie earned his Field Champion title in 2005 and became a nationally ranked dog, earning us an invitation to participate in the prestigious Buckeye Invitational Field Trial with the top twenty field champion Dachshunds in the country. He won the fifth annual Buckeye Invitational in 2007 and repeated his spectacular win in 2008. As his owner, handler, and trainer, I couldn't be prouder, but nothing makes me happier than seeing his tail wagging when I come through the door at day's end.

—*Sherry Ruggeiri, field trial handler*

Dachsies are active dogs, so they should be given the chance to burn off some energy with a doggie sport.

RALLY BEHIND RALLY

Rally is a sport that combines competition obedience with elements of agility, but is less demanding than either one of these activities. The sport was designed for the average dog owner in mind, and is easier than many other sporting activities.

At a rally event, dogs and handlers are asked to move through ten to twenty different stations, depending on the level of competition. The stations are marked by numbered signs, which tell the handler the exercise to be performed at this station. The exercises vary from making different types of turns to changing pace.

Dogs can earn rally titles as they get better at the sport and move through the different levels. The titles to strive for are Rally Novice, Rally Advanced, Rally Excellent, and Rally Advanced Excellent.

To get your Dachshund puppy prepared to do rally competition, focus on teaching basic obedience, for starters. Your dog must know the five basic obedience commands and perform them well before he's ready for rally. Next, you can enroll your dog in a rally class. Although he must be at least six months of age to compete in rally, you can start training long before his six-month birthday.

SHOW DOGS

When you purchase your Dachsie, make it clear to the breeder whether you want one just as a companion and pet, or if you hope to be buying a Dachsie with show prospects. No reputable breeder will sell you a puppy and tell you that he is definitely of show quality, for so much can go wrong during the early months of a puppy's development. If you plan to show, what you will hopefully have acquired is a puppy with show potential.

To the novice, exhibiting a Dachshund in

Before You Begin

Sports are demanding physically. Have your vet do a full examination of your Dachshund to rule out joint problems, heart disease, eye aliments, and other maladies. Once you get the all-clear health-wise, start having fun in your new sporting life!

SMART TIP!

the show ring may look easy, but it takes a lot of hard work and devotion to garner a win at a show such as the prestigious Westminster Kennel Club dog show, not to mention a little luck, too!

The first concept that the canine novice learns when watching a dog show is that each dog first competes against members of its own breed. Once the judge has selected the best member of each breed (Best of Breed), the chosen dog will compete with other dogs in its group. Because each coat variety competes separately at dog shows, the Dachshund has three shots at winning the Hound Group in every show. No other breed has three shots at winning its group! Finally, the dogs chosen first in each group will compete for Best in Show.

The second concept is that the dogs are not actually compared against one another. The judge compares each dog against his breed standard, the written description of the ideal specimen that is approved by the AKC. While some early breed standards were based on specific dogs that were famous or popular, many dedicated enthusiasts say that a perfect specimen, as described in the standard, has never walked into a show ring, has never been bred and, to the woe of dog breeders around the globe, does not exist. Breeders attempt to get as close to this ideal as possible with every litter, but theoretically the perfect dog is so elusive that it is impossible. (And if the "perfect" dog were born, breeders and judges probably would never agree that it was indeed perfect.)

Do you have what it takes to get in the ring? The show ring, that is.

If you are interested in exploring the world of conformation, your best bet is to join your local breed club or the national (or parent) club, which is the Dachshund Club of America. These clubs often host regional and national specialties, shows only for Dachshunds, which can include conformation as well as obedience and field trials. Even if you have no intention of competing with your Dachshund, a specialty is a like a festival for lovers of the breed who congregate to share their favorite topic: Dachshunds! Clubs also send out newsletters, and some organize training days and seminars so people can learn more about their chosen breed. To locate the breed club closest to you, contact the AKC, which furnishes the rules and regulations for all of these events, plus general dog registration and other basic requirements of dog ownership.

Dachshunds are just one breed that can compete in earthdog trials. Do you want to dig deeper and find out what other breeds are eligible for this sport? Go to **DogChannel.com/Club-Dachsie** and click on "downloads."

JOIN OUR ONLINE
Dachsie
Club

My first Field Champion was a miniature wirehaired Dachshund named Buzz, the runt of the litter, who was a longshot even to survive. But Buzz was a fighter and survived.

When I first met Buzz as a puppy, it was love at first lick; we immediately understood each other. He was this alert, little ball of wirehaired energy wanting to please me, and waiting for a job. I could only laugh with amazement at how cute this underdog was. Soon my life would be forever changed.

Like his Field Champion parents, Buzz loved to work and loved the praise from a job well done. Thus, he was an ideal candidate for the task he was bred to do: rabbit scenting.

Our bond grew as we began field training. We both thrived on teamwork. I would handle him to the place where a rabbit had run from, and he would put his nose down and work the scent line's curves and turns until he found the rabbit hole. Then, I would pick up Buzz and praise him for all his good work. That's when he started to make a humming noise—he would "buzz" with a contented excitement.

Our training began to pay off. His first ribbon was a first place in Rhode Island, and he defeated every dog he was braced with. Buzz quickly earned enough points to become a Field Champion. But competing now with the top field champions in the country would be daunting—for him and for me. And winning? Well, that would be a longshot again.

But Buzz kept winning. He worked with tremendous accuracy and precision. He knew we were a team, and he never wanted to let me down. The only thing more powerful than his nose was his loving heart.

Then one day day during a field trial, Buzz became oddly tired. I noticed he had also cut himself on a thorn. I picked him up, and held him up see more closely. He wouldn't stop bleeding, and my jacket was drenched with blood. I took him to the vet immediately, and they ran a myriad of tests. He had a very low platelet count, so his blood wouldn't clot. For two weeks, he fought for his life, and again survival was a longshot.

At home, I gave him much-needed rest. But because Buzz lived for his scenting job, I had to gently let him practice or he would get depressed and his condition worsen. For three years, we kept a balance. Then he became well enough to work through earthdog tunnels to scent out caged rats.

He couldn't wait to get back to field trials, and neither could I. One morning at a field trial in Pennsylvania, Buzz was braced against Oscar, the

number one Field Champion in the country for seven years. And yes, winning over Oscar would be like David defeating Goliath.....this would be the complete and total longshot.

And, by some miracle, little Buzz won. And he went on to become the Absolute Winner, the top prize at a field trial. That was one of our proudest moments.

Three weeks later, after a weekend scenting rabbits in Ohio, Buzz's little

9-pound body wore out, and he died in my arms. He died doing what he loved to do. I could not wish anything better for my hero. He taught me to fight, to never give up and to reach for goals when others thought they were impossible to achieve.

Buzz was my "forever dog," and he left this world on a star. And that's a long, long way from being a longshot.

—John Merriman,
field trial judge and handler

Dachsies can swim (top left), excel at agility (top right) and hunt (left). They're multitalented hounds!

For more information about this breed, contact the following organizations. Their members will be glad to help you dig deeper into the world of the Dachshund.

American Kennel Club: The AKC website offers information and links to conformation, tracking, rally, obedience, and agility programs and member clubs: www.akc.org

American Working Terrier Association: The AWTA has earthdog information. www.dirt-dog.com

Canadian Kennel Club: Our northern neighbor's oldest kennel club is similar to the AKC and the United Kennel Club in the States. www.ckc.ca

Dachshund Adoption and Rescue: This nonprofit organization is dedicated to rehoming homeless Dachshunds. www.daretorescue.com

Dachshund Club of America: The Dachshund Club of America website features articles, show results, pictures, breed, local club, membership information, and more. www.dachshund-dca.org

Dachshund Rescue of North America: DRNA is an organization for rescuing, rehabilitating and rehoming needy Dachshunds and Dachshund mixes. It is a network of rescuers throughout the United States and Canada. www.drna.org

National Miniature Dachshund Club: The NMDC has all the Dachshund information you need—in miniature form! www.dachshund-nmdc.org

North American Dog Agility Council: This site provides links to clubs, trainers and agility trainers in the United States and Canada: www.nadac.com

North American Teckel Club: The mission of the NATC is to preserve the Dachshund's hunting heritage, to promote their usefulness in the field and to support the breeding of Dachshunds with sound bodies and stable temperaments. www.teckelclub.org

United Kennel Club: The UKC offers several of the events offered by the AKC, including agility, conformation and obedience. In addition, the UKC offers competitions in hunting and dog sport (companion and protective events). Both the UKC and the AKC offer programs for juniors, ages two to eighteen: www.ukcdogs.com

U.S. Dog Agility Association: The USDAA has info on training, clubs and North American events and overseas: www.usdaa.com

BOARDING

So you want to take a family vacation—and you want to include all members of the family. You probably would make arrangements for accommodations ahead of time anyway, but this is especially important when traveling with a dog. You do not want to make an overnight stop at the only place around for miles and find out that they do not allow dogs. Also, you do not want to reserve a room for your family without confirming that you are traveling with a dog because, if it is against their policy, you may not have a place to stay.

Alternatively, if you are traveling and choose not to bring your Dachshund with you, you will have to arrange accommodations for him. Some options are to bring him to a neighbor's house, to have a trusted neighbor stop by often or stay at

it's a Fact

A big part of socialization is merely exposure. Give your puppy the opportunity to hear the whoosh of hydraulic brakes on city buses and take in the rattle and stench of garbage trucks, while learning that nothing bad happens as a result of those sounds, sights and smells.

your house, or to bring your dog to a reputable boarding kennel.

If you choose to board him at a kennel, you should visit in advance to see the facilities provided, how clean they are and where the dogs are kept. Talk to some of the employees and see how they treat the dogs—do they spend time with the dogs, play with them, exercise them, etc.? Also find out the kennel's policy on vaccinations and what they require. This is for all of the dogs' safety since, when dogs are kept together, there is a greater risk of diseases being passed from dog to dog.

HOME STAFFING

For the Dachshund parent who works all day, a pet sitter or dog walker may be the perfect solution for the lonely Dachsie longing for a midday stroll. Dog owners can approach local high schools or community centers if they don't know a neighbor who's interested in a part-time commitment. Interview potential dog walkers and consider their experience with dogs and your Dachshund's rapport with the candidate. (Dachshunds are excellent judges of character, unless there's liver involved.) Always check references before entrusting your dog and home to a new dog walker.

For an owner's long-term absence, such as a three-day business trip or a week-long vacation, many Dachshund owners welcome the services of a pet-sitter. It's usually less stressful on the Dachsie to stay home with a pet sitter than to be boarded in a kennel. Pet sit-

SMART TIP!

Remember to keep your dog's leash slack when interacting with other dogs. It is not unusual for a dog to pick out one or two canine neighbors to dislike. If you know there's bad blood between your dog and an oncoming dog, step off to the side and put a barrier, such as a parked car, between the dogs. If there are no barriers to be had, move to the side of the walkway, cue your dog to sit, stay and watch you until his nemesis passes; then continue your walk.

ters also may be more affordable than a week's stay at a full-service doggie day care.

Pet sitters must be even more reliable than dog walkers, as the dog is depending on his surrogate owner for all of his needs for an extended period of time. Owners are well advised to hire a certified pet sitter through the National Association of Professional Pet Sitters, which can be accessed online at www.petsitters.org. NAPPS provides online and toll-free pet sitter locator services. The nonprofit organization only certifies serious-minded, professional individuals who are knowledgeable in behavior, nutrition, health, and safety. Always keep your Dachshund's best interest at heart when planning a trip.

SCHOOL'S IN SESSION

Puppy kindergarten, which is usually open to puppies between 3 to 6 months of age, allows puppies to learn and socialize with other dogs and people in a structured setting. Classes help your Dachshund enjoy going places with you, and help your dog become a well-behaved member of public gatherings that include other dogs. They prepare him for adult obedience classes, as well as for life.

The problem with most puppy kindergarten classes is that they only occur one night a week. What about during the rest of the week?

If you're at home all week, you may be able to find other places to take your puppy, but you have to be careful about dog parks and locations where just any dog can go. An experience with a bully can undo all the good your classes have done, or worse, end in tragedy.

If you work, your puppy may be home alone all day, a tough situation for an energetic Dachshund. Chances are he can't hold himself that long, so your potty training will be undermined unless you're just aiming to teach him to use an indoor potty. And chances are, by the time you come home, he'll be so bursting with energy that you may start feeling he's hyperactive.

The answer? Doggie day care. Most larger cities have some sort of day care, whether it's a boarding kennel that keeps your dog in a run or a full service day care that offers training, play time, and even spa facilities. They range from a person who keeps a few dogs at her home to a state of the art facility built just for the purpose. Many of the more sophisticated doggie day cares offer webcams so you can see your dog throughout the day. Look for:

- escape-proof facilities, including buffers between the dogs and any doors
- inoculation requirements
- midday meals for young dogs
- obedience training (if offered), using reward-based methods
- safe and comfortable resting areas
- screening of dogs for aggression
- small playgroups of similar sizes and ages
- toys and playground equipment, such as tunnels
- trained staff, with an adequate number to supervise the dogs (no more than 10 to 15 dogs per person)
- webcam

Puppy classes will introduce your Dachsie to other dogs (real ones, not just his stuffed animals!).

CAR TRAVEL

You should accustom your Dachshund to riding in a car at an early age. You may or may not take him in the car often, but at the very least he will need to go to the vet and you do not want these trips to be traumatic for the dog or troublesome for you. The safest way for a dog to ride in the car is in his crate. If he uses a crate in the house, you can use the same crate for travel.

Another option is a specially made safety harness for dogs, which straps the dog in much like a seat belt. Do not let your dog roam loose in the vehicle—this is very dangerous! If you should stop short, your dog can be thrown and injured. If the dog starts climbing on you and pestering you while you are driving, you will not be able to concentrate on the road. It is an unsafe situation for everyone—human and canine.

For long trips, be prepared to stop to let your Dachshund relieve himself. Take with you whatever you need to clean up after him, including some paper towels and perhaps some old bath towels for use should he have an accident in the car or suffer from motion sickness.

Did You Know? The dog run is one of the few urban spaces where a dog can be off-leash. To enter most dog parks, dogs must be fully vaccinated and healthy, and females must not be in season.

IDENTIFICATION

Your Dachshund is your valued companion and friend. That is why you always keep a close eye on him and you have made sure that he cannot escape from the yard or wriggle out of his collar and run away from you. However, accidents can happen and there may come a time when your dog unexpectedly gets separated from you. If this unfortunate event should occur, the first thing on your mind will be finding him. Proper identification, including an ID tag, a tattoo and possibly a microchip, will increase the chances of his being returned to you safely and quickly.

An ID tag on a collar or harness is the primary means of pet identification (and ID licenses are required in many communities, anyway). Although inexpensive and easy to read, collars and ID tags can come off or be taken off.

A microchip doesn't get lost. Containing a unique ID number which can be read by a scanner, the microchip is embedded under the pet's skin. It's invaluable for identifying lost or stolen pets. However, to be effective, the chip must be registered in a national database and owner contact info kept up-to-date. Additionally, not every shelter or veterinary clinic has a scanner, nor do most folks who might pick up and try to return the lost pet.

Best bet: Get both!

Did You Know? Some communities have created regular dog runs and separate spaces for small dogs. These small dog runs are ideal for introducing puppies to the dog park experience. The runs are smaller, the participants are smaller and their owners are often more vigilant because they are used to watching out for their fragile companions

INDEX